FROM THE PUBLISHER OF Antique Trader

FANTASTIC FINDS

·········

FROM AUCTIONS TO YARD SALES, REAL-WORLD STORIES OF ANTIQUE DISCOVERIES

Copyright ©2011 F+W Media, Inc.

Published by

Krause Publications, a division of F+W Media, Inc.
700 East State Street • Iola, WI 54990-0001
715-445-2214 • 888-457-2873
www.krausebooks.com

To order books or other products call toll-free 1-800-258-0929
or visit us online at www.krausebooks.com

Photos on the front and back covers represent the Fantastic Finds found within the book. Shown on the front, clockwise from left: *Showcase* #4 (Oct 1956) featuring the first revival of The Flash; carnival glass mid-size vase in Tree Trunk pattern, aqua opalescent; Nancy J. Morris with her solid-metal bank sign (see story on P. 154); a Mickey Mouse toy; a Tiffany lamp; a steamer trunk. **Shown on the back cover, from the top**: a "personality" hat (see story on P. 4); a Shawnee Muggsy cookie jar (see story on P. 29); a book of photographs of early Hawaii (see story on P. 18); a green Depression glass plate (see story on P. 54); and a 1949 Cadillac (see story on P. 166).

ISBN-13: 978-1-4402-3056-1
ISBN-10: 1-4402-3056-0

Designed by Sharon Bartsch
Edited by Kristine Manty

Printed in the United States of America

CONTENTS

Every collector has tales of amazing discoveries, yard-sale surprises, and life-long hunts that lead to ultimate treasures. These are the stories told on the fields of Brimfield and in the auction galleries before the first gavel falls. In 2009, *Antique Trader* magazine launched its Favorite Finds contest. We asked our readers to share these memories in hopes they would inspire a new generation of collectors. Three years later, the response is still overwhelming. Readers are sending stories from every corner of the country, sharing their discoveries and greatest finds. One fellow learned his $700 auction gamble was a $38,500 sapphire bracelet. Fan favorites include a junk-shop find worthy of Sotheby's, rare garage-sale comic books, and a Navajo rug snagged for $5.

Not all of these finds are valuable in the traditional sense. Then again, value, as an antique collector often defines it, takes many different forms, most of which are personal.

My favorite find is something most people would probably never consider worth keeping, let alone worthy of cherishing. Juxtaposed with my love of Midwest folk art and American art pottery is my fascination with Depression- and World War II-era hats children made from their fathers' cast-off fedoras. I first discovered these at a Baltimore antiques show. Resting on a top shelf was an old gray fedora with its brim neatly trimmed in a zigzag pattern. The hat was covered with dozens of celluloid gumball prizes, pinback buttons, Cracker Jack charms, toys and odd bits and pieces a child would have found on his daily adventures. I picked up a few of these 'beanie' hats over the years, but only by chance. I never sought more with any serious effort.

Five years later, I was browsing an online shop by chance when I came across another one of these hats. Covered with key chains and political and novelty pinbacks from Sweet Caporal Cigarettes, this hat retained a scrap of a vintage Boy Scouts of America patch, a Rutgers college button and even a plaque with a patent, a serial number and Chinese characters off of a Victor

Talking Machine. I marveled at the variety of objects and thought about the kid who scrounged up all these odds and ends and liked them well enough to ask his mom to sew them on his dad's old hat. Maybe he traded other trinkets to assemble his collection. Maybe these items were the only things the boy owned outright. I bookmarked the hat's webpage and went back to work.

Whenever my workday got particularly tense, I clicked the link and visited the hat. I don't know why its odd assemblage melted stress away or why this particular item became my virtual "happy place." I visited the hat off and on during the course of an entire year. One day — it wasn't there! Gone! Had it sold? Who else would want it? Where's my hat?

I contacted the seller and learned that after an item posted on her website records a certain number of views and does not sell, it is automatically removed. The dealer said she often wondered who was viewing the hat so many times — over and over again — during the last year but still hadn't purchased it. We shared a laugh that I racked up enough visits to cause the hat to get removed from the site. We worked out a price, and that hat still makes me happy every time I see it.

The stories you'll find in this book are like that. They represent the most personal connection between the treasure hunter living inside every collector and the objects we adore —no matter their monetary value. We hope you enjoy these tales of the hunt and fateful discoveries ... and we hope you consider sharing your fantastic find someday. Who knows. Yours may just be the right one to inspire a new generation of treasure hunters.

We welcome more stories. Each submission must include the author's full name, address, and a telephone number or e-mail address. Send your entries to Antique Trader Favorite Finds, 700 E. State St., Iola, WI 54990 or to atnews@fw-media.com or fax: 715-445-4087. If sending by e-mail, please include the words 'Favorite Finds' in the subject line of your message.

Many thanks goes to the readers and followers who graciously and generously share their memories every year. Thanks to editors Kris Manty and Susan Sliwicki and designer Sharon Bartsch for their time and talent.

– Eric Bradley, Editor of *Antique Trader*, www.antiquetrader.com

CHAPTER 1

BOOKS
AND
COMICS

ROYCROFT BOOK COLLECTOR
FINDS HISTORICAL RARITIES

· · · · · · · · ·

I became an avid collector of books published by the Roycrofters, East Aurora, N.Y., in 1978. On a Thursday evening in 1986, a few minutes after I got home from work, the phone rang.

The caller told me his name, and said, "I'm in New York visiting my son, and

I brought along a trunk full of Roycroft books hoping to sell them. But none of the dealers I spoke to were interested. One of them suggested that I give you a call." My first thought was that if none of the New York dealers was interested, then why should I be.

However, I was courteous and asked if he could give me an idea of what he had. The first book he mentioned was *Ali Baba*, a nice book. The second was also good. Then: "And this one's called '*The Bibliomaniac* ... ' "

I froze.

A book by that name had been listed in one of the early Roycroft catalogs, but I knew of no institution or collector who had a copy. Now he really had my attention. He then went on to list a few more titles, all better than average: limited editions, illumined, etc.

I said I was interested, and perhaps we could set up an appointment. We arranged to meet at 9:30 a.m. that Saturday at his son's apartment. I did not sleep well the night before.

Friday evening, I arrived home fully expecting to find a message on my answering machine saying that he had a change of heart and decided to keep the books, or, one of the dealers he had contacted had a change of heart, or ... well, you collectors out there are familiar with those nervous rushes — when you're sure you're going to lose something you desperately covet.

Saturday arrives. After sleeping only lightly, I finally gave up, got up about 5 a.m., fussed around a little, got dressed, hit the road about 7 a. m., and got to his son's building at 8:30.

I waited until 9 and, with the impatience typical of the biblio-mad, rang the bell. He opened the door after what seemed like another eternity, dressed in pajamas and a bathrobe. We climbed up five flights to the apartment.

The place was dark, sparsely furnished, and I had the distinct feeling that there were several people still sleeping somewhere in it. We sat on the floor (yes, floor) next to a large suitcase. He opened it and proceeded to hand me Roycroft books one at a time.

The first was the *Ali Baba*, an exceptional copy. The next was also a limited edition, in equally fine condition. And next ... he handed me the *Bibliomaniac*.

It was a smallish, suede-bound book with a water stain on the cover. I noted immediately that it had a wallet (leather) edge signifying a book of some distinction. The title page was typical and dated March 27, 1908. The following page had a cryptic dedication and then I turned to the next page. I read (to myself) and froze — again! "Of this edition only two copies were printed of which this is No. One."

It was a few moments before I was able to unclench my eyes and teeth, defense mechanisms necessary to help stifle the rising scream that would surely have awakened the building. "This is really terrific," I heard myself squeak.

A few more books ... observed in a daze. Then ... he handed me another suede-bound, wallet-edged book titled *A Myth* by A.N. Idlyr, obviously a pseudonym. I had never heard of this book.

The first blank leaf bore an inscription and was dated March 27, 1907, (note: this date is exactly one year prior to the publication date of "*The Bibliomaniac*"). The title page was hand-illumined, and then I turned to the next page. I had some hair back then, and the apartment was still pretty dark, so the Krakatoan eruption of sweat from the top of my head probably went unnoticed. I read, "Of this edition only two copies were printed, of which this is No. One."

I said that I wanted to buy all the books, and made an offer that I felt—I hoped—he couldn't refuse.

Would he respond with the dreaded, "Sounds good; let me think it over for a few days," or "I'm waiting for another offer, and I'll let you know," or...?

"OK," he said.

He accepted!!! His son, now awake, helped me carry the books down to my car, and I drove home to Connecticut on this late morning of a beautiful fall day — at about 4 miles per hour.

— **Richard Blacher**
via e-mail

P.S.: During conversation, the seller told me that he had recently sold "The Inn at Stone City" (Iowa), which he had purchased and refurbished several years before. The Inn had originally been Grant Wood's famous Art Colony, active in the summers of the early '30s. The books had been found stored in Grant Wood's apartment.

Oh, yes, and I sent the New York dealer who referred him to me a very nice gift.

OUR RETIREMENT COURTESY OF YOUR FRIENDLY NEIGHBORHOOD SPIDER-MAN

· · · · · · · · ·

In 1980, my husband and I were living in Lincoln, Neb., with our young son. We did not know a soul as we were recently transferred there.

The only pastime we could afford was frequenting garage sales, and we main-ly looked for toys or books for our son. At one sale we came across boxes full of hundreds of comic books. We negotiated the price to about a nickel each and hauled them to our apartment.

Upon closer examination, we realized we might have made a wise investment, but not for our son's entertain-ment. We had purchased *Action Comics, Batman, Fantastic Four, Journey into Mystery, Sgt. Fury, Thor*, etc. We took a couple of the lowest-numbered items to a comic book dealer, as we knew just enough to be dangerous. He was honest and kind enough to provide us with a few protective sleeves, and his hands shook just a bit as he placed one in particular into its protective covering. When we purchased a guide from him and started cataloging what we had, we realized the reason. Though not in great condition, this comic was *Amazing Spider-Man No. 1.*

We are now considering selling our collection. We are nearing retirement age, and I believe we should realize more than we invested all those years ago!

— **Terry Niehaus**
City withheld by request

Buck Rogers helped a lot of kids become interested in science fiction and fascinated them with anti-gravity gadgets, rayguns and moon flights.

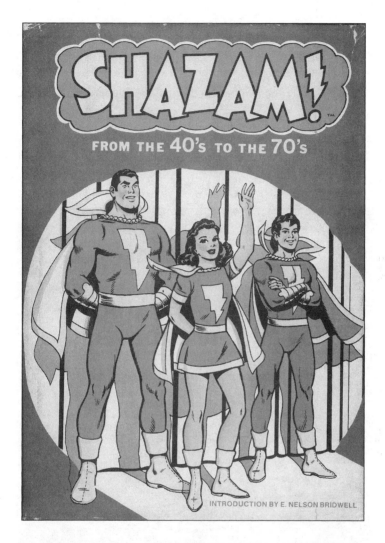

LONGTIME COMICS COLLECTOR
FINDS TREASURED BOOKS

· · · · · · · · ·

When I was growing up, reprint collections of comics were few and far between. Yes, there were a few paperbacks collecting such newspaper strips as
Peanuts, but they usually weren't complete, and there seemed to be no interest
in maintaining continuity. The true treats were such volumes as Jules Feiffer's

"*Great Comic Book Heroes*," Stan Lee's "*Origins of Marvel Comics*" (and its sequels), and DC's "*Secret Origins of the Super DC Heroes.*"

I also rabidly devoured Bonanza Books' trio of hardcovers — collecting dozens of stories featuring Batman, Superman and The Marvel Family, respectively, from the '30s, '40s, '50s, '60s, and '70s. In addition, I enjoyed the oversized hardcovers that collected such newspaper strips as *Buck Rogers* and *Little Orphan Annie. The Smithsonian Collection of Newspaper Comics* introduced me to many strips I hadn't seen before.

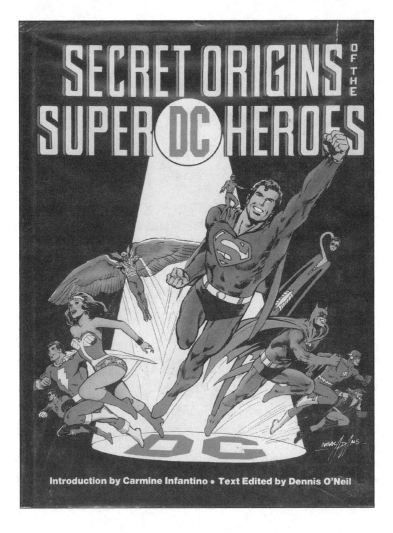

The only problem was that those were pretty much the only offerings I could find. My local library had several magazine holders with individual comic books (which put me way ahead of the game compared to kids in many other towns) but didn't often restock them, and there didn't seem to be many other sources.

I've been an avid comics collector and reader for more than 40 years. As part of my collection, I wanted to have my own copies of those big ol' books I used to take out of the library. Through several instances of being in the right place at the right time, I've picked up nearly all of them. My copy of Feiffer's book came

THE GREAT COMIC BOOK HEROES

The origins and early adventures of the classic
super-heroes of the comic books—in glorious color.

Compiled, introduced and annotated by

JULES FEIFFER

with a bonus: a number of comics-related newspaper articles neatly clipped and tucked inside the front cover. After years of searching, I finally received a copy of *"Shazam! From the Forties to the Seventies,"* which is one of my most treasured possessions. An online auction yielded both a hardcover and a softcover copy of *"Secret Origins of the Super DC Heroes,"* while a warehouse sale garnered me the *Buck Rogers* and *Little Orphan Annie* books.

— **Brent Frankenhoff**
Editor, *Comics Buyer's Guide*
http://cbgxtra.com

ONLY 'THE SHADOW KNOWS' THIS FELLOW WANTED THESE PULPS

· · · · · · · · ·

The great article in *Antique Trader* titled "Pulp Revival" (Aug. 4, 2010, edition) jogged my memory and prompted me to write about "our find."

On a beautiful fall morning in east-central Iowa, my wife and I decided that an auction was a great way to spend the day. There were two farm auctions within a few miles of each other with lots of good stuff.

Arriving at the first farm, we set out looking on the tables and hay wagons, and then headed for the rows of boxes on the ground. In one dilapidated box was an assortment of old schoolbooks, an old *"Farmer's Almanac"* and maybe something else; I can't remember.

But what did catch my attention was something from my childhood. As many young people born in the 1940s, radio played a big part in our growing up. There, under the miscellaneous books, were dozens of *The Shadow* paper dime novels in near-mint condition. I could not believe it. He was my favorite radio sleuth.

I really wanted to get to the other sale because they had an old school bell like we had been wanting in our yard. So we split up, and I told my wife to bid that box up to maybe $30 or $40.

The bell went too high for my blood, and I headed back to see how well she had done. When I got there she had her stash in one pile, and among it was the box full of books. I was overjoyed and asked her how much she had to pay. With a big smile she replied: $11. And to boot, the guy that bid her up offered her $5 for the almanac. What makes this story good was that our oldest son was heading off for college and we needed some money. By looking in the *Antique Trader* classifieds we located a man advertising for dime novels. We sent him one as an example of the quality and got together on a price. That is the first time we ever turned $6 into $1,000. We still go to auctions, and we still are looking through boxes hoping to make another "big find."

— **Gary Whitmore**
Osceola, Mo.

READER'S FAVORITE FIND HAS HOLLYWOOD TIES

• • • • • • • • •

I found my favorite find more than 10 years ago on a trip "out East" with my husband and both our moms. We were on Route 6, I think, in Pennsylvania, in a little antiques store. There, in a small back room, on a magazine rack, tucked almost out of sight, I found a printed collection of letters, pages tied together with a strip of suede. The printed title caught my eye, "Letters from Mr. Wu, Toto and General Byng to Mr. and Mrs. Albert L. Grey." Someone had written "To L" in ink on the cover. The pages were folio-sized, thick, with ragged edges. The title page was beautifully printed in black and red Gothic text. I saw the price, $4, and bought it without even opening it up, thinking that it might be fun to share with everybody as we drove along.

When we were on the road again, I took out the collection of letters and began to read aloud, "Printed by J. Miles & Co., London, Printers to His Majesty the King." That got everyone's attention! Another page yielded this information: "This Edition is limited to 12 copies, of which this is No. 8." The real excitement, though, was in the content of the letters: They came from an address in New York and were written to "Mummy" or "Daddy," by Mr. Wu, Toto and General Byng," who — we determined many miles later, and to our utter delight — were the family's three dogs, "writing" to their "parents," who were away on a trip in London. Those letters still intrigue me: I wonder to this day who actually wrote them, who paid to have them printed, and who might have received those other editions, in addition to "L," whomever that is! Some of the pages had outlined boxes printed, and I am sure photos were meant to be attached within ... Were they of Albert and Almah, or photos of the family dogs?

But after hours of research, I did finally discover who Mr. and Mrs. Albert L. Grey were. My research of the New York address (which is still in existence, by the way) led me to an ocean liner that had traveled to New York from Cherbourg, France, in the 1920s, with Albert L. and his wife, Almah, on board, along with Albert's brother, David Wark Griffith! That's right, Albert was the brother of the famous American film director, D.W. Griffith!

All these years later, I am still researching that collection of letters, trying to find out more about the Greys and their connection to J. Miles in London. I have found, for instance, that J. Miles & Co. printed pantomimes, theater bills and some of the music used in D.W. Griffith's films. I found out that Almah was from Australia and married the then-30-plus-year-old Albert when she was just 19. I found out that Albert was D.W.'s manager for a time and even published his own (albeit short-lived) film magazine. Whatever happened to Albert and Almah I don't know; they lived large but went bankrupt in the 1930s, and she later traveled to Italy as an opera singer. I have found Albert's short obituary, but I have never found hers.

I value my collection of letters so much more now than when I bought them. Then, they were a novelty—something to read aloud on a long car ride—but now, I keep them with no small sense of reverence. It's almost as if the more I learn about these people, the more I want to keep their memories alive. They lived and breathed, laughed and cried, had money and lost money, lived and died. Those letters make their lives real to me. Their stories aren't yet complete.

And so, if your readers have any information about my collection of letters, or the Greys, or J. Miles & Co., I hope they will write in to *Antique Trader*.

And the search continues ...

— **Karen Edwards**
Michigan

PROGRAM REVEALS SIGNATURE OF BASEBALL GREAT

• • • • • • • •

My favorite find this year almost didn't happen. I almost never shop at antiques malls because I have a shop myself, and it's hard to buy for resale at mall prices. But I had helped a friend set up a garage sale on a rainy Saturday and had an hour or so before my store opened, so I ran into an excellent mall near my friend's house, just to take a quick look. In a dealer's booth, I found a little folded program, undated but professionally printed, "Chicago Cubs vs. Waukegan High

School Faculty." Odd that these should be juxtaposed, I thought. And the dealer had clearly marked its container, a clear plastic bag, "Cubs autographs, $5."

Sure enough, four members of the team (which I later determined had to be 1968 or so) had signed the back of the program. I couldn't make out all the signatures, but one positively leaped out at me: Ron Santo, long beloved by Chicagoans, so recently deceased that his memory has been lauded incessantly in the last year, and a sure-fire candidate for the Baseball Hall of Fame, according to Cubs fans.

A couple of the other signers (I eventually deciphered them) also became quite well known later on, but Santo was the clincher. The upshot? I sold the program — within a couple of days — for three figures! (I don't want to say exactly how much just in case the buyer or his friends read this.) Certainly proof positive that you just never know what you're going to find—and where you're going to find it!

> — **Bindy Bitterman**
> **Eureka! Antiques of Evanston, Ill.**

DUMPSTER DIVING UNCOVERS VALUABLE PHOTOGRAPHS

· · · · · · · · ·

For years I have gone to garage sales and flea markets and been Dumpster diving. I have found many unique items but never anything worth more than about $100 — until that day I spied a box of books in a Dumpster in one of our local parks.

I have always liked old books, so I fished around and pulled out several books that looked interesting and took them home.

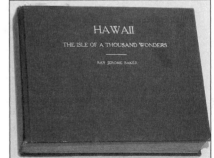

A few days later, when I finally got around to looking at my finds, one book especially caught my eye. It was a book

Ray Jerome Baker

of black-and-white photographs of early Hawaii (1939) by Ray Jerome Baker. The more I examined it, the more unique it looked. It was published by the photographer himself, not by a publishing house. The pictures weren't prints of photographs, but actual bound photographs.

The more I looked at it, the more interesting it appeared to be, and the more I thought it might be worth maybe as much as $100.

One of the photographs in the book.

Another photograph in the book.

Photos courtesy Artfact.com

I went to several rare book sites on the Internet, but no luck. No one had a copy for sale. Dead end. I put the book aside until the day I received a pair of tickets to the "Antiques Roadshow."

I had always wanted to go to "Antiques Roadshow" and take some of my finds, but what to take? I looked at that book again and decided it would be fun to find out if it was really worth something as I hoped. I had told several friends that I thought I had found something really good and was about to find out.

At the "Roadshow," I approached the appraisers' table with great anticipation, already revising my value estimate up to $220 or $300. At first he didn't seem impressed and couldn't find the book listed on his computer. He tried another website and suddenly closed his laptop and said he couldn't tell me anything more until he talked to the show's producer, Marsha. "I knew it. It has to be worth something if he has called for the producer," I thought. I revised my estimate up to $500 or maybe even $1,000.

The real value of the book for me was just beginning. It was the experience of going through the "Roadshow" process of being interviewed, taped, and six months later finding out that your segment actually made it on air that was priceless. The fact that the book was appraised for $5,000 to $6,000 didn't hurt, either. It certainly turned out to be the Holy Grail for a Dumpster diver, putting me and my find on "Antiques Roadshow."

Presently I have no plans to the book, because it keeps on giving. Friends keep on asking to see it and hear the story. People are constantly mentioning how they saw me on "Roadshow" and ask about the experience. I even find that I now appear in several spots on the Internet and even now have a chance to be published in this *Antique Trader* book. What more could one ask for?

— **Martin Stoye**
Santa Roas, Calif

IS POPE LEO XIII CATHOLIC? SURE! BUT IS THIS HIS SIGNATURE? WE'LL SEE

· · · · · · · · ·

My 2011 find is an antiquarian book. It is not just any book; it is dedicated and signed by Pope Leo XIII. My dilemma is to authenticate the signature as Pope Leo XIII or someone close to him at The Vatican who would be able to sign it for him, as often is the case. It is rare to find a book signed by a sitting Pope out of the hands of the family originally given the book.

I acquired the book from a book dealer who probably did not read or speak German, but he sells many books written in foreign languages. It was just my lucky day to be looking in that section of the bookstore. I picked up a number of foreign language books that day and bought some in French, Chinese and, of course, German. I did not have any soul music that day, so I put together an

An inside page.

eclectic mix of divine literature.

The book signed by Pope Leo XIII is a Catholic school language book, and I am investigating how this book could have received a rare signature of a Pope. The book began its journey from Wisconsin, I believe, as a written name in the book says, but that is open to interpretation. The student's name is also there, so that helps in my quest to unravel the rest of the odyssey of this journey. I have already contacted the Milwaukee Archdiocese for assistance in determining if there was an official travel mission to the Vatican in the 1870s-1880s, and an ecclesiastic book dealer has kindly consented to translate the dedication for me. The question is: Did Pope Leo XIII sign the book himself, or another cardinal/bishop at the Vatican? I am eagerly waiting to hear from those I contacted to find out. Intuitively, I believe the dedication and signature are authentic to Pope Leo XIII.

— **Sharon D. Smith**
Los Angeles, Calif.

THE PRIZE GOES TO THE HIGHEST BIDDER, BUT THE HUNT IS HALF THE FUN

· · · · · · · · ·

I want the snapping turtle shell. The runners keep passing it by in favor of small pottery and attic paintings as they thread their way through a cramped space full of furniture and people sipping coffee. Everyone is dressed in sweatshirts and jeans, belying the money that seems to fly around the room when a juicy item is proffered. I almost bid on the 150-pound anvil, but decide against it and head out into the rain to eat a hot dog. My wife, Amy, will fight for the shell if it comes up.

We're at Roberson's Auction House in Pine Bush, N.Y., on a Saturday in Octo-

From Charles Ives' *114 Songs*.

ber. Last night in the charmingly rustic Blackberry Barn on the other side of the Shawangunk Ridge, we built a fire and read books to the sounds of Sibelius on an old record player. Squirrels in the eaves of the barn skittered on the roof, trying to keep out of the rain. Amy roasted marshmallows as we sipped hot toddies. It was a weekend made for antiquing.

However, we eschewed antiques stores for the more frenetic pleasures of the auction house. No doubt most of the others here were dealers, and the prices for much of the merchandise was steep. Still, the chance to match wits and wallets with the hobbyists and collectors gave both of us more enjoyment than overpaying in one of the Hudson Valley antiques shops. We had enjoyed antiquing in the past but rarely bought anything beyond a book or two. We just didn't have that kind of money and didn't know enough to find a bargain on anything except literature. But even used bookstores often disappointed us with prices far beyond what a 50-year-old paperback should bring. Then, we discovered the joys of auctions.

The runner yelps, pointing out a bidder to the auctioneer. Estate jewelry is hot today. We haven't bid on anything yet, but now the shell goes up. The dealer starts bidding at $100, though he mentions what an "odd item" it is. He drops to $25, and two of the sweatshirted women begin to bid, passing me by at $45. We thought no one would want such a strange piece, but I guess it would look neat in the window of a shop. I could probably find one in the mud of the nearby river if I really wanted one. So why were we here? The table in the corner that would look good in our foyer?

We had experienced our first auction at Nest Egg in Meriden, Conn. The huge auction hall and clear auctioneer, not to mention the fun, family atmosphere, all endeared us to the experience. We bid on and bought a few bins of ancient books. The next time, we picked up an office chair and a telescope.

Then, we had reserved our own table for an open auction. We laid it out with rock 'n' roll records, comic books, a collection of old coins and an Oriental rug my mother donated to the cause. Nervously, we waited while the pros sold their knickknacks and glassware. Finally, our table was up, and the coins began to go fast, one lot selling for $140. The rug went for $50, though no one seemed to value the comic books, which I figured were by far the most expensive lot. Still, the table brought in $400, twice what we had paid out at Nest Egg so far. This was a new level of excitement.

A month later, Nest Egg had a fantastic book auction, mostly the library of Hearthstone Castle in Danbury, Conn. We browsed the lots of hardbacks, bidding on 20 or 30 lots, getting some Sir Walter Scott, Louisa May Alcott and a huge set of original Hardy Boys. We snatched up cheap lots of paperbacks full of books I actually wanted to read.

But it was one of the small lots, interesting 19th-century poetry bought for $5, that would bring us joy. Plugging these strange tomes one by one into the Internet, I found them worth $5, $10, $30. Then I plugged in the oddity of the lot — composer Charles Ives' "*114 Songs*." Immediately it showed up for sale at $1,750. I checked and double checked the volume. It was genuine, and moreover signed by Minnie Ives, the songwriter's sister-in-law. Ives was from Danbury, and his family lived in the same circles as the Hearthstone Castle people.

I knew I couldn't get full price for it, but I e-mailed a dealer in antique music, who offered $1,000 on inspection. A week later. we had the check and they had the book to sell for twice that. We had our moment of luck, and it hooked us. Now, we were here on vacation in the Gunks, and a rainy day was the perfect time to visit the local auction house.

We only win a stained glass window and a pair of milk pails at the Pine Bush auction, leaving for a few tastings on the Shawangunk Wine Trail. But someday, maybe we'll find the next $1,000 first edition, $10,000 Civil War rifle, or $100,000 Connecticut impressionist painting. Maybe not. But along the way we could pick up some inexpensive antique teapots and a rustic coffee table for our house. Plus, the hunt is fun, the bidding exciting, and the hope of victory sweeter than the prize. I didn't need the turtle shell after all.

— **Eric D. Lehman**
English Department
University of Bridgeport
Bridgeport, Conn.

"KEY COMICS"

Here is some expert advice when on the hunt for valuable comic books, taken from "*Comics Shop*," published by Krause Publications:

So-called "key comics" are historically significant comics. That is to say, they contain such events as: the first appearance of a character; a major change in that character's life; or a new concept, such as putting several heroes together as a team.

Scarcity and demand can also play into determining a key issue. While the horror, crime and science-fiction comics produced by E.C. Comics in the early 1950s are highly sought after by

many collectors, the real keys (in terms of scarcity) among all that publisher's releases are the file copies stored away by owner William Gaines at the time and made available to the public in the 1980s.

Gaines' file copies are also an example of another factor that can determine a key issue: a pedigree. Pedigrees are typically granted to collections that can be identified as belonging to a single collector, who amassed his collection by purchasing his comics from the newsstand, preserving those comics carefully and retaining many key or rare comics in that original collection.

The most famous of such pedigrees is the Mile High Collection, amassed by Colorado commercial artist Edgar Church in the 1930s and 1940s and discovered by Chuck Rozanski in the 1970s when Church's heirs were clearing the artist's home. Other well-known pedigree collections include (but are not limited to) the Allentown Collection, the Larson Collection, and the Bethlehem Collection.

Since many super-heroes were introduced in the late 1930s and early 1940s, there are many key comics from that time. In addition to Action #1 and Detective #27, other keys of that era include Marvel Comics #1 (Nov 39, first Human Torch, first Sub-Mariner), Detective Comics #38 (Apr 40, first Robin), Superman #1 (Sum 39), Batman #1 (Apr 40), All-Star Comics #3 (Win 40, first teaming of heroes, in The Justice Society of America), All-Star Comics #8 (Jan 42, first Wonder Woman), and Captain America Comics #1 (Mar 41).

WHAT IS CGC?

CGC is the abbreviation for Certified Guaranty Company, an independent grading firm that evaluates comics, gives them a condition grade based on strict criteria and a 10-point scale, and then encapsulates the comic book in a hard plastic holder with the grade prominently displayed. This independent grading levels the playing field for buyers and sellers by establishing a grade that both can agree on and trust.

For more information, prices and identification on comic books, read "*Comics Shop*" by Brent Frankenhoff, Maggie Thompson and Peter Bickford available at Shop.Collect.com or 800-258-0929.

CHAPTER 2

CHINA
AND
POTTERY

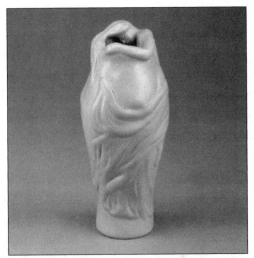

For more on this Fantastic Find, see page 43.

COLLECTOR SURVIVES THE GREAT COOKIE JAR RUSH OF '09

• • • • • • • •

One of the great joys of collecting cookie jars is the hunt. Nothing gets the heart beating faster than seeing a long-sought jar tucked away in the corner of an antiques store or sitting on a kitchen counter at an estate sale.

Recently, we joined other collectors and dealers on a hunt at an estate sale about three hours from our home in southern California. Unlike the majority of estate sales, this one allowed you to sign up early to hold your place in line, but there was a catch. There always is. The sign-up list went up at midnight, but you couldn't leave and come back the next morning for the sale. You had to stay with your car, parked on the street, except for one 30-minute run in order to fetch coffee or find a bathroom. If you left and didn't come back, your name was scratched off the list.

So why did we decide go? Because we saw in one of the online pictures a portion of a blue bow that could only be a 1940s Shawnee Muggsy cookie jar. After confirming with the company handling the sale that there were more than 60 cookie jars being offered, we knew we had to join the hunt.

My partner, Gary, and I arrived at the location at 11:20 p.m., and when the list went up, we were Nos. 10 and 11 on the list.

We had brought along pillows but two six-foot tall, middle-aged men aren't going to find comfort in a Saturn Ion coupe, no matter how hard we tried. As it was a humid night, we left the windows down, and at 3 a.m. we enjoyed an unexpected shower compliments of the home's sprinkler system!

By 4 a.m., there were 66 people signed up, and when dawn broke, the list had climbed to 120 names.

Emblazoned on the gate of the estate sale home was "Tara," and sure enough, the home behind the gates was a smaller version of the famous mansion from "Gone with the Wind." In fact, the entire neighborhood had thematic homes. Across the way was a Mediterranean villa next door a South Seas estate. One further down the road had been styled after the Greek Acropolis. What a setting

The Shawnee Muggsy jar.

for an estate sale.

We mingled and chatted with fellow collectors to determine our competition. There were at least three other cookie jar collectors, but they were further down the list, so our chances looked good.

At 7:30 a.m., they lined us up and gave us final instructions not to run, push, punch, grab or steal. Precisely at 8 a.m., they opened the gates, allowing the first 25 people down the hedge-lined path to the open front doors. I didn't run, but I'm 6 foot, 3 inches and can stride past the best of them, even if my legs were still cramping from a night spent in a shoebox-sized car.

Hoping the jars were in the kitchen, I traversed the front steps in a single bound, crossed through the front doors past a grand staircase into a dining room where I could see in the reflection of a mirror the jars sitting on a kitchen table.

Hearing footsteps and panting behind me, I lengthened my stride and reached the cookie jar-laden table first.

As it turned out, the panting was coming from Gary, who started placing cookie jars into our boxes as if possessed. We didn't check condition, as we knew we could do that later in a holding area. We just grabbed and placed the jars in our boxes and about our feet.

By the time we had 16 cookie jars on the ground, two collectors had made it to the table. Their groans confirmed we already had the best jars, but that didn't stop one determined collector from trying to reach for the Shawnee Muggsy. Politely, but firmly, she was told the jar was sold.

"How much?" she inquired.

"Forty dollars," I replied, raising myself to my full height indicating she would need more than herself to wrestle the $450 book-valued cookie jar away from me.

Then the real fun began.

We had to take each jar from the kitchen to the holding area, circumnavigating what had now become a crazed mass of overly tired and anxious buyers. With sounds of breaking china in our ears, we carried all 16 jars to a holding table, carefully avoiding one poor lady who had slipped and fallen on a small set of steps. As she was already being helped, we didn't stop. Besides, it could have been a diversionary tactic.

After careful inspection, we returned nine jars to the kitchen because their condition was not acceptable. We still had to get seven cookie jars and two salt and pepper sets through the front doors, across a long veranda and down six steps to the checkout tent on the driveway — all the while avoiding Grand Central Station-type crowds.

I carried the first two jars to the check-out tent, leaving Gary to guard the jars on the holding table. He was now 200 yards away from me, and that one lady collector was still buzzing about him, determined to run off with at least one of the jars.

A lady we had chatted with before the sale started came to our rescue, and among the three of us, we guarded and carried until the jars had been placed in the checkout tent and been paid for.

Taking turns, we carried them to our car. When the last jar had made it safely into the car, we leaned back on the trunk and watched in amazement the scene before us. I can only describe it as if one were watching a colony of army ants flowing in and out of their hill. Some carrying items, others scurrying about in search of treasures, and yet more pressed hard against the front gates, still trying to get in.

When the dust had settled, we had in our car the Shawnee Muggsy for $40, a McCoy's Boy on a Baseball for $12, Kitten in Basketweave and Dog in Basketweave for $25, a Metlox Mammy for $55, a Sierra Vista/Starnes Froggy Goes a Courtin' for $12, a Brayton Laguna Mammy for $65, and two sets of Muggsy salt and pepper shakers, one plain and one gold, for $8 each. It was a successful, exhausting, exhilarating hunt we will never forget. Would we drive three hours and sleep in our car again just to buy some cookie jars? You bet! Because it is this type of magical, crazy adventure that makes collecting so much fun and so worthwhile.

— **Brian Parkinson**
Desert Hot Springs, Calif.

ONE COLLECTOR'S LOSS IS ANOTHER'S HEIRLOOM

• • • • • • • •

One beautiful spring Saturday a few years ago, I was doing some random garage-sale stopping. I was in a neighborhood of middle-class, cookie-cutter homes. The usual stuff was scattered in the driveway, but then, at the rear, there was a sheet spread out with a funny china set. Well, not really a set, just odd pieces; they were all painted with flowers and most had little bugs painted on the pieces. I turned one piece over, and the mark was like a pair of crossed golf clubs.

I was captivated by the bugs and puzzled by the mark. The woman wanted $50 for all, and then she showed me it included more pieces, all in an old cardboard box covered with dust and mouse droppings inside everything. The woman said the pieces were her aunt's. They didn't match her pattern.

Her grown daughter was helping her mom with the yard sale, and the mother gave the daughter one last chance to hold on to old Aunt Polly's china. The girl declined, and I bought the pieces. I didn't haggle, because I felt it was a fair price. As I was walking back down the driveway, box in hand, not knowing what I had, behind me walked an older couple, the husband was chewing out his wife quite loudly. "Next time you see something like that, don't come and get me, just buy it," he sternly lectured her. I realized that I had the box of china that he probably wanted. For a moment, I thought, 'I'll bet I could sell this to them for $100 and make a quick profit.' But then, I liked the bugs and wanted to go home, look in my book of china marks and find out if the crossed golf clubs were in the book.

I came home and washed the tea pot up. It was cute, with a little rosebud on the lid. I found the mark in the book. Oops, not crossed golf clubs, crossed swords. The pieces are all very old Meissen/Dresden. Looking with a magnifying glass, I could tell there were no transfers; these were really all hand-painted pieces. There were 40 pieces in total: the pride of my china cupboard.

Although one young lady rejected her aunt's china, my daughter has told me never to sell them; they are her inheritance.

— **Elizabeth DeYenno**
via e-mail

JUNKING HUNT LANDS
THE REAL MCCOY

· · · · · · · · ·

I'm always on the lookout for a good deal, particularly when it comes to antiques and collectibles. I hit yard sales, consignment shops and second-hand stores on a regular basis. Even though I may not always find a treasure, the hunt is always fun. In fact, the hunt is usually the most fun part. And I only buy what I like — the golden rule of collecting.

Every July, during our town's annual car show, yard sales abound. Anyone with anything to sell hauls it into a garage or onto a front lawn, and the crowds throng. This past July was no exception. And, of course, I was part of that crowd!

What total fun. Prowling about with my sister, another junking junkie, we scoured one sale after another. We found the usual odds and ends, but nothing remarkable. Then, on a dusty table in a far corner of someone's garage, I spied what looked like a lovely McCoy vase for a mere $4. It sat amid several other

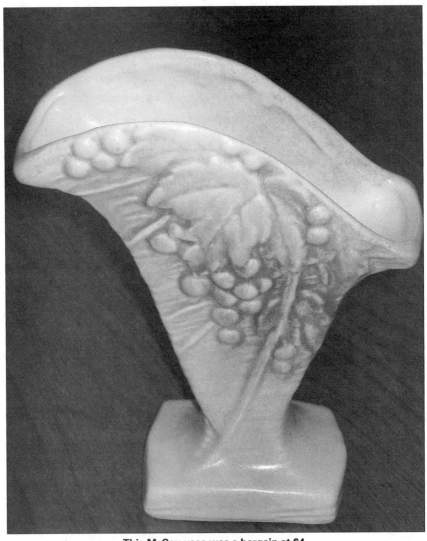

This McCoy vase was a bargain at $4.

labeled collectibles with much higher price tags.

"It can't be McCoy," I thought. "The price would be higher if it was McCoy." No mark on the bottom, but I knew some McCoy items aren't marked. "But it's a bargain at $4," I thought. "I like it. It will look nice in my kitchen, and if it is indeed McCoy, so much the better. I don't have any McCoy pieces in my collection … yet!"

Sure enough, after I got home and did some investigating, I discovered it is, indeed, a McCoy Rustic Grape pattern vase. It now has a place of pride in my kitchen.

— Mary Sieber
Iola, Wis.

BUYER REMAINS COOL
AND WALKS OFF WITH HOT VASE

• • • • • • • • •

A half a dozen years ago, a co-worker, Doug, and I traveled up to Atlanta on business. In the afternoon after our business was over, we rode over to an area on the north side of town where a group of antiques/collectibles shops were located. I was on the lookout for my favorite collectible, McCoy Pottery. Although Doug

The uncommon maroon-glazed McCoy vase.

had a passing interest in McCoy, his specialty is mugs with military emblems or slogans on them.

It had been a long time since I visited the area, and my hope of finding a "goodie" was high. But after looking through a couple of shops, the picking didn't look too promising. I saw a fair number of McCoy pieces, but none that I didn't already have.

We were about to leave the third shop when I spotted a foot-tall vase sitting on the floor. It was tucked against the wall, between to shelving units, and nearly unnoticeable due to a large crock sitting in front of it. As soon as I saw it, I recognized it as an unmarked McCoy.

The vase is uncommon, and it is one that I had been seeking for a long time.

I knew that I wanted this type vase, but right then my job was to examine the vase for damage. There was none, so now the question was how much the dealer wanted. As the dealer approached, I talked to him with my negotiating phraseology.

I asked, "How much do you want for this thing?" I didn't want to give the vase any important status, or give the impression I really wanted it no matter what.

The dealer responded, "$80."

I halfway mumbled, "I can't give you that much."

I must have caught the dealer at the right time, because he asked, "Well, how much will you give me?"

Although I didn't need to, I paused for a minute or so, still playing a somewhat disinterested person.

I finally said, "I could give you $60." He said, "OK," and the deal was done.

When we left the shop, I told Doug how proud I was that I was able to get this uncommon vase, particularly in the rare maroon glaze it had. He wanted to know what kind of deal I got.

I told him it was difficult to know exactly, but I thought the vase was worth a couple of hundred at least. Man, was I surprised to learn at an auction sometime later that this very same style maroon vase sold for $1,100.

During my nearly 30 years of collecting McCoy pottery, there is one thing I have learned: Always persevere, because it pays off. You can never tell when or where you will run across some special piece that you have been searching for.

— **Dewayne Imsand**
Mobile, Ala.

LETTER CARRIER FINDS RARE HALLS POT

• • • • • • • •

I am an avid collector of cookie jars, Halls china, general store and soda fountain just to name a few. I am also a letter carrier, which is an excellent job to help contribute to my large collection.

One day I had a certified letter for a customer. She asked me to step inside and she then apologized for the clutter due to her impending garage sale. My eyes focused on an extra large Lipton ice tea pot on a very large base, with a spigot on the front.

The bottom was printed "Halls China." She said it was a presented to her grandfather who was a vice president of the Lipton Tea Company. I never saw anything like it before, and I really wanted it. I asked her if it was part of the sale and she agreed to sell it if I wanted it.

By this time my mind was going a mile a minute. She asked how much I was willing to offer. I knew it was worth a lot so I replied "How about $50?" She accepted. "Would you like to take it with you?" she asked. I thought about it, but I was afraid it might break in the truck. I told her I would be over after work to get it.

After work I quickly drove over to her house to get it. When I arrived she was standing outside of her house shaking her head at me. I thought to myself she either found out how much it's worth or talked to someone else who knew the value of the tea pot. I wondered why didn't I just take it with me earlier when I had the chance. When I got to the top of the steps she said, "I'm sorry but I can't just do it." My heart sank to my toes. She looked at me and said, "I can only charge you $20." I kept a straight face, said thank you and took it home.

The tea pot has been on my kitchen nook table ever since, and to this day it remains the pride of my collection. I have never seen another one like it — ever!

— **Harry Kaplan,**
via e-mail

HIDING UNDER THE GRIME
WAS A FAVORITE FIND

· · · · · · · · ·

Somehow, I never really got into "garage sales." Being a teacher, I was never able to go on Friday when most sales began, and I supposed all of the bargains would be gone by evening. Also, the only time I could sleep late was Saturday mornings!

So one Friday afternoon, as I left school for home, I could see from the street a tall glass pitcher at a garage sale. As I love any kind of pitcher, I stopped to check it out. To my dismay, the pitcher was very badly damaged. However, right beside the damaged pitcher was a small, round Hull bowknot basket in the matte finish.

At that time I was avidly collecting Hull pottery. The basket had evidently been stored in a basement for many years and had several layers of dampness and dirt.

I actually couldn't tell if it was cracked or damaged, but for $5, I couldn't pass it up. To my delight, after a bath in warm soapy water, it turned out to be perfect. I have seen it sell twice at auctions for over $300! That was about 25 years ago, and it remains my favorite find, even though I have been retired for 16 years and can be the early bird at garage sales if I so desire.

— **Della Ellingsworth**
via e-mail

GARAGE SALING YIELDS A STEAL
OF A DEAL ON A METTLACH STEIN

· · · · · · · · ·

It was Saturday, garage sale day! I was moseying around the West Bank of New Orleans, checking off good possibilities from the *Times-Picayune*, one of which was the yard sale of a fellow Marine wife who was downsizing their accumulated stuff.

We military wives often do that, like every time we get permanent change of station orders. The reason is simple: Uncle Sam has a weight allowance we must be under, or the cost can be in the thousands of dollars. We don't make that kind of money ... so we offload our treasures.

You develop a system when you cruise sales. Well, most of us do, or else we would not be able to hit many sales. I was letting my eyes float over tables of items when they stopped at a beer stein. Now, I had collected the Budweiser Holiday Steins from the early 1980s, but this one was different. It rang a bell like a five-alarm fire in my brain. Somewhere that little half liter stein ... I looked again. It was German. I sidled up to the table and reached over for a pick-up look-see. Running my fingers over the cameo-like figures, the name Mettlach jumped into the headlines of my thinker. I turned it over, and there it was, the telltale mark of Villeroy & Boch, the castle. Sheesh! A Mettlach beer stein at a garage sale? With shaky fingers I turned the tag over to see the price: $50.

Hmmm, that's couldn't be right. I got the lady's attention and asked about it. It was the correct price. "Um," I said, "I'm not up on German beer steins, but when I was stationed there, I couldn't afford to even look at a Mettlach stein. You might want to have someone who is up on them take a look at it."

Now, you might say, "Hooey, what a dummy. She's got a wowser of a deal and she's tossing it away?" But my mindset is we have to help each other. If this person was a dealer in a shop and selling it for peanuts, I would figure, "Hey, they are in business and must not care." But when someone who is obviously not in the know and selling stuff so hubby can go to school or because they need the money, well, I figure the right thing is to advise them that they should try to get it appraised or checked out. If they don't, then I'll pay their price and sleep like a baby.

The seller said someone else had told her it could fetch more, but that was what she wanted. "Would you take a check?" I asked, since 50 bucks was more than I carried back then. "No checks," she replied.

"Would you hold it for $5 'til I go home and get some more cash?"

"OK," was her answer.

I flew out of there like a scalded skunk. Back to the apartment, up the 14 steps double time and burst through the door like a shot.

"Doug! Doug!" I hollered for my hubby.

"Wha … Wha ..." He groggily sat up in bed (He's a night owl, I'm a chickadee).

"QuickIneedfiftydollarsforaGermanbeerstein!"

"WHAAA? Slow down! Start over!"

Then he fixed me with "The Look." It's a Marine thing. I think they start practicing it in front of the bathroom mirror around the time they make staff sergeant so when they attain the rank of Gunny, all they have to do is give you "The Look" and you shrivel up or turn tail and scram. I stopped dancing from foot to foot, took a deep breath and explained my need.

"And you woke me from a sound sleep for that?" he rumbled while flopping back down on the bed. But before his head hit the pillow, I heard him say, "Help yourself, it's over there," he said, waving his hand in the direction of his wallet.

I had the money and was out the door and gone before he could even snore. I backtracked to the beer stein sale and parted company with the cash. I didn't even haggle. I had my very own Mettlach, Villeroy & Boch beer stein! YOWZA!

— **Kathleen Melville-Hall**
Alpena, Mich.

DOLLAR LOT REVEALS EARLY POTTERY

• • • • • • • • •

It was one of those rare fall Sundays in southern Wisconsin. The sun was shining, the maples and oaks were at the peak of color, and the urge to spend an afternoon outdoors was overwhelming. There were no mosquitoes nor gnats to fight; only one bug had bitten us — the auction bug. Giving in, my husband and I succumbed to the pull of the auctioneer's gavel.

It was a common household auction with nothing outstanding listed. The tables were laden with the usual glassware, books, pottery and assorted effluvia. There was so much "stuff" that there were two auctioneers in two rings.

My husband stayed in the back of the house to bid on some old sheet music — not exciting to me, so I wandered to the front of the house where the action was more scintillating. I have to admit, to my hubby's chagrin, that I am one of those people auctioneers love. I cannot resist the "one dollar for it all" bid.

I was busy packing up a table full of bargains when he returned from the back of the house, his sheet music in tow. His general attitude toward my newly purchased table full of items was simple: "If all it takes is $1 to keep you happy, go for it!"

Later that afternoon, as I unpacked and inspected my auction boxes, I was serenaded by my husband on the piano to the strains of "Hard Hearted Hannah" and other vintage sheet music selections. His musical treasures were about to become secondary to mine! In my pile of crockery and glassware, I found a little brown pottery bowl with an etching on the bottom that read 'Ceramic Arts Studio.' There was also a signature inscribed in the clay, but I couldn't quite make it out. A little research led us to a website for the Madison Ceramic Arts Studio of Madison, Wis.

The company was founded in 1940 by Lawrence Rabbitt, a University of Wisconsin student who studied Wisconsin clay for pottery-making purposes. The studio produced figurines, shelf sitters, head vases and other ceramic pieces from 1940 to 1956. There were many potters who worked for the company during its history, but Rabbitt was the first. The name jumped out at me as I was doing my research. Rabbitt! That was the signature on the bottom of the bowl. I had an early signed piece from the studio. Rabbitt left the studio in 1942, so he had only two years of actual production time with the firm.

I took the bowl to a pottery show in Madison a few years ago and an expert there authenticated the signature. I am happy to know it's valued at about $350 by the collectors of Madison Ceramic Arts Studio pieces, but the historical significance of the piece and my acquisition of it makes it priceless.

Needless to say, my hubby no longer questions my impulsive bidding. So to all my kindred auction junkies, keep in mind that a hidden treasure may be only a gavel strike away.

— **Barbara Willoughby**
Evansville, Wis.

YARD SALE YIELDS A ROSEVILLE WALL POCKET FOR POCKET CHANGE

• • • • • • • • •

Thinking back to some of my favorite finds at yard sales:

1. About 10 years ago, digging through a box at a yard sale, I found a Hull "teacup" wall pocket for 50 cents. It was vintage Hull, not reproduction.

2. Four or five years ago at a carport sale (sitting on a little metal shelf) was a vintage Roseville wall pocket. I believe it is the Wisteria pattern, pretty blueish green with creamy yellowish flowers. It was in absolutely mint condition for $1. Roseville is inscribed on the back of the wall pocket with the original price sticker, which has faded and is now blank. This was fairly exciting, needless to say!

3. About 8 or 10 years ago, driving down one of our local streets, I saw a house that I had never seen a yard sale at. I was tired and nearly drove off because all I could see from my car was clothing — not what I wanted! But something told me to check it out, and up the walk I went. On the porch, not visible from the street, was a box with two brown stoneware mixing bowls in it and two Fire King Jadeite swirl mixing bowls with original price tags attached — all four bowls for $2.

I believe these are three of the main reasons I look forward to yard-sale season each year. I've collected for 30 years and been an antique dealer since 1992. I LOVE the thrill of the hunt. I have enjoyed sharing these memories with you.

— **Paula Hall Flora**
via e-mail

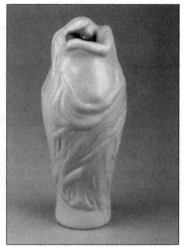

The lamp that was really a vase, with authentic mark, at left.

BARGAIN HUNTER COULDN'T RESIST THE SIREN SONG OF THIS LORELEI

• • • • • • • •

I frequent yard sales and flea markets but can't always, and don't always, feel the need to beat the sun out there. On this particular Sunday, I was walking around the local flea market at about noon when I spotted a lamp. It was sporting an ugly, crooked burlap shade, but the base was smooth and bulbous and a lovely turquoise color.

I didn't know if it worked, but including the light bulb, it cost me a dollar. When I got home, I showed my husband, and I said, "This looks like the same color as the Van Briggle vase you bought."

You see, several years ago my husband came home from his early Saturday morning excursions and presented me with a beautiful pottery vase. I fell in love with it because it was in beautiful shades of turquoise and the surface was so smooth and nice to touch. It has a matte finish and a lovely jonquil or daffodil molded up the entire side of the vase. The vase is signed on the bottom Van Briggle — and if you've ever seen a Van Briggle or held one, you know exactly what I'm talking about.

Well, as his eyes glazed over, he took the lamp from me and in short work proceeded to dismantle it. Besides the burlap shade, it had a cardboard tube (of the paper-towel variety) sprayed gold and inserted in the neck to hide the electrical works.

It turned out to be a vase, a vase with a name of Lorelei by Van Briggle. After the shade and tube were removed, you could see her face and realize that it was her entire body wrapped around the length of the vase ending with her tiny sculpted foot. This is my most excellent find.

— **Roxan Schneider**
Bensalem, Pa.

HOUSE CLEANOUTS REVEAL HIDDEN TREASURES

• • • • • • • • •

When both of my parents passed away in '96, the wife and I got the tedious job of cleaning out the house — what to keep, what to throw.

My wife was in favor of throwing out just about everything. My mother was a pack rat who never threw out anything — post cards to holiday cards; letters; record collections that reached into the thousands; you name it — even *TV Guides*.

Reading *Antique Trader* for some years, I was able to recognize that some of this stuff had value. Convincing the wife was another thing. If I had listened to her, I would not have found the $50 inside an anniversary card. At that point, I went through everything.

The real find was a vase with very faint markings on the bottom. I tried taking a rubbing without much effect. Turning into the light just so, to cast a shadow, I could make out a very faint "Red Wing USA" with numbers or lettering on the bottom.

There was a free antique appraisal in town, and it confirmed my finding was correct: It was Red Wing, black gray with white speckles, it measures 9-1/2 inches high, the base 2-3/4 inches wide by 2 inches high. There is a small line crack running down the inside, probably during firing, but not visible on the outside of the glazing. I have read and seen a lot of Red Wing items but never anything like this. I would guess to say it is one of a kind.

Some years back I was cleaning out my mother-in-law's attic with family members, trying to keep ahead of things being thrown away, when we came across a wood framed print of "The Unanimous Declaration of the Thirteen United States of America. In Congress, July 4, 1776." It has an old wood panel backing and measured 31-3/8 inches high by 24-1/2 inches wide. No one wanted it, so I put it in a pile of stuff I was taking.

On the bottom it read "Published for Sale by Humphry Phelps, No. 144 Fulton St., near Broadway, N. York."

I think I counted 57 signatures on the lower half, with John Hancock being the most recognizable. I had a local auctioneer give me an appraisal of only $35. I thought that was somewhat low. So I decided to write to a New York and Boston Auction House and again I got two different values. One had no interest and the other thought it was worth $1,000 to $1,500.

So I feel I'm back to square one. I was hoping you or some of your readers could shed some light and put an end to this cat-and-mouse game.

— **Charles Williamson**
Gloucester, Mass.

FAVORITE FINDS SMALL BUT DEAR

· · · · · · · · ·

Here are pictures of some of my finds in the past couple years. The candleholder I purchased at a Goodwill store, the iron-handled sunflower item at a church sale and the koala bear we have had for some time.

Teddy bear.

Iron-handled item.

Candlestick

I don't know the origin of the bear, and I don't know what the iron-handled item was used for.

— **Richard Daub**
Indianapolis, Ind.

A POTTERY PICKER'S DREAM COME TRUE

•••••••••

I'm lucky enough to have a cottage only 45 minutes from home. When I go up for the weekend, I can't wait to go garage-sale hunting. It expands my hunting grounds considerably.

I found one of my regular stops open on a Saturday morning. This is a garage sale that is set up in a garage and is open almost every other weekend. As I walked in the garage, I saw a whole shelf of Uhl pottery. I have collected Uhl for more than 25 years, and there before me was enough to double or triple my collection.

There were five shelves full and a wall unit with a bunch of ceramic mugs. I could hardly wait to gather up as many pieces as I could afford at the moment and asked if they were going to be open on Sunday. As I was told "yes," I was already trying to think of what I was going to tell my wife. She took it well, and even loaned me some of her "stash money." This scenario went on for five or six visits over the next month until I had pretty much cleaned up. Altogether I accumulated nine egg cartons and probably 200 pieces. It was a picker's dream come true. I still have a hard time believing someone else didn't find this treasure trove. The garage-saling couple told me twice: "You really made our day," and I told them, "You made mine, too!"

On another day in July 2011, I went out hunting on a bright, sunny Saturday morning, as is the norm. About five blocks from home, I found a small group of neighbors on a park strip along a boulevard having a sale. I walked around a few of the tables full of knickknacks and noticed across the table from where I had just left was a brown Brush-McCoy onyx vase (valued at approximately $75). It was full of artificial flowers, and that is what camouflaged it from the opposite side of the table. The vase was marked $5, and I couldn't unload the flowers fast enough. The best part of the find was, as I stepped out of my car to cross the street, there was a $5 bill lying in the street!

— **Dave Myers**
Fort Wayne, Ind.

SIGNIFICANCE OF CROWN-MARKED HUMMEL WAS LOST ON BUYER

• • • • • • • • •

In the late 1960s, I purchased a small, 4-inch Hummel, "The Merry Wanderer," for $5. It contained the "Crown" marking on the bottom, which I didn't know the significance of at that time. Subsequently, I noticed its greater value from my Hummel book. Today, its market value has come down, but it's still worth hundreds of dollars.

— **Edith Peterson**
Speculator, N.Y.

GLASS

Pioneer, crystal luncheon plate, fruit center.

THE MORE DEPRESSION GLASS, THE MERRIER FOR THIS COLLECTOR

• • • • • • • • •

I love to troll consignment shops and second-hand stores for antiques and collectibles, and sometimes I'm lucky. Last summer, I scored some Depression glass at my local Goodwill store.

Depression glass is one of my all-time favorites. I love all the different colors and patterns. To me, nothing's quite as lovely as a dinner table sparkling with Depression glass. The first item I found, an amber dinner plate in the Madrid pattern, was just sitting on an open shelf mingled in with all the pedestrian glass castoffs — not even behind the counter where the store normally displays its more valuable items. For less than $5, I walked out with a treasure. On another occasion I bought a green Cherry Blossom saucer, perched on a clearance end-cap, for 99 cents!

But my most memorable Depression glass moment was when we disposed of my mother-in-law's estate. My husband and I were fortunate to end up with her Depression glass. There weren't a lot of pieces, but they were all in excellent condition, and we were delighted to get them: Colony sugar bowl, creamer and olive

Sharon, pink 10-1/2" fruit bowl.

dish; Miss America celery dish; Old Colony salad bowl; Pioneer luncheon plate; Sharon fruit bowl. We display them proudly in our china cabinet and use them on special occasions. We will eventually pass them on to our son.

— **Mary Sieber**
Iola, Wis.

Old Colony Lace Edge, pink 7-3/4″ d salad bowl.

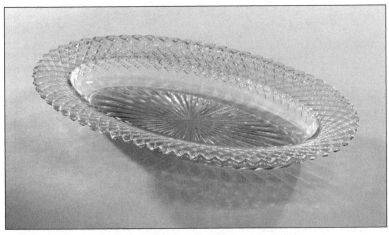

Miss America, pink 10-1/2″ oval celery dish.

Colony, crystal 7" olive dish.

Colony, crystal sugar; crystal creamer.

$7 KITCHEN BOX LOT HID
A DEPRESSION GLASS TREASURE

· · · · · · · · ·

I really enjoy auctions and am always looking for something to add to my collections. I have several, among them glass baskets (250), clear glass creamers (200) shot glasses/toothpicks (200) children's milk mugs (150) and salt dips/salt cellars (300). I am not interested in duplicates, so it is getting hard to find items to add to the collections.

I also enjoy buying box lots that almost every sale has at the very end of the sale. You never know what "treasure" you will find when you get home and sort through the muddled mess.

Several years ago I attended a local auction. I did not find anything to add to my collections but decided to wait around for the box lots, which I could see were going to be near the end of the sale.

One lot consisted of a great variety of old kitchen utensils, but instead of being in a box, they were all in a large glass bowl. There were several items that I could not identify and this made me desire the lot even more. Bidding was slow by that time, and I purchased the lot for $7.

When I got home, I dumped out the bunch of old-fashioned can and bottle openers, paring knives, measuring spoons and cups, granny three-tine forks, melon ballers and assorted unknown items.

After washing all the utensils, I washed the large clear glass bowl. Was I surprised when I found the mark in the bottom, a diamond with the H in the center — the HEISEY mark!

I have a number of Heisey pieces in several of my collections and also have in my library a book on Heisey pieces. I looked this item up and found it to be a punch bowl from the 1920s, and the value at that time was between $75 and $100! What a find for my $7 investment.

Happy hunting for that unknown treasure at your next auction.

— **Beverly Miller**
Middlebury, Ind.

WHO SAYS GAMBLING DOESN'T PAY OFF?

· · · · · · · · ·

Years ago, my husband and I were staying in a small hotel in the Catskill Mountains and decided to get into a poker game. After a few hours, we were elated to find that we won $600 between us.

We left to go home, and on the way, we noticed a small antiques shop on a deserted country road. As soon as we walked in, we both spotted this beautiful fixture signed "Daum Nancy." The price, miraculously, was $600. We decided to buy it. Last year, we decided to put it up for auction, as we were redecorating. The darn thing sold for $7,000. A pretty good investment, I'd say. Happy antiquing!

— **Rhoda Satenspiel**
Boca Raton, Fla.

FAVORITE FIND COMBINES BIRTHDAY AND POTTERY

· · · · · · · · ·

Many years ago, we had a booth at the Lucadia Flea Market on old 101 in California (before Carlsbad, Calif.), and another dealer wanted to sell his booth and all the contents. The price was right, and husband and I just wanted that spot.

There really wasn't too much Depression glass, which I specialize in, but many smalls that would be OK with the glass. My favorite find of my life was the Bauer 4-1/2-inch Cobalt Christmas and New Year's plate for 1928 — the year I was born. Shock for me of course, I've kept it all these years (still in mint condition). I'll be 83 come March 1, 2011.

I am still in a mall and enjoy it still.

— **Hazel Stewart**
Winfield, Kan.

$3 YARD-SALE BUY WAS A SUPER-RARE HEISEY

••••••••

At a yard sale, my brother-in-law Steve found what appeared to be a crystal vase approximately 12 inches high and heavy. He paid $3. Upon further inspection, we determined the mark was Heisey. I looked in my books, but it was not in any of them.

"Put it on eBay!" Steve said. I started it at $19.99 and it sold for $403.05!

After the auction, a Heisey Glass Museum officer contacted me and asked for permission to use my pictures. He said it was a rare piece from the 1940s and even the museum did not have one to display. Needless to say, I'm hooked!

— **Darlene Fishell**
Surprise, Ariz.

A LIFETIME OF MEMORIES, AND CAKE

••••••••

Perhaps it was while vacuuming up generations of spiders and cobwebs in the basement. Or maybe it was while filling the driveway Dumpster with decades-old junk from the garage. It could even have been while gashing my leg moving an impossibly heavy highboy down impossibly steep steps.

No matter. Somewhere along the way, the warm recollections that fueled my early efforts were gone. Sifting though my parents' belongings was no stroll down memory lane. It was a hard, frustrating and seemingly endless job.

Nostalgia was out the window, along with three boxes of musty Sports Illustrated magazines from my childhood that I had saved in that spider-infested basement.

My parents — God rest their souls — came from humble stock, experiencing the Great Depression firsthand as children. They knew the value of a dollar and the potential of almost anything, so they saved. Almost everything.

We live in a mobile society. We change addresses as often as we do our minds

— and sometimes as quickly. My parents, however, did not.

They built their home in central Wisconsin some 60 years ago. They took root, making a life there and raising five children. I am the youngest. It is the only home the family knew. It may seem odd today, but my parents had only one telephone number their entire life together. I have had at least 15.

My father passed away this summer. He was 91. My mother died nearly 10 years earlier. They had a good life, modest but filled with family, friends and laughter. And, it seemed, paper bags, jars, string, boxes and almost anything that one day might be useful. There were photographs, letters and cherished cards. Decades worth. And those were the good things to go through, until they weren't.

This Florentine No. 2 green Depression glass plate holds special memories.

Until even the most cherished were just another load to be dealt with.

And so it went. A lot was saved, much was given away, and even more was tossed. Nostalgia is for those who can afford it, I told myself as I gave the heave-ho to yet another bag of their memories. I grew tired and cranky. This was crazy. I was spending too much time and way too much energy disposing of things my parents held on to. Why didn't they let go? Why couldn't they have done this so we wouldn't have to? What were they thinking?

I got my answer in the form of a Depression glass plate. My sister found it, and, pulling me aside from the rest of the family, gave it to me. "This is for you," she said smiling. "Mom would have liked you having it."

It was the plate my mother placed our birthday cakes on. Each year, as a treat befitting birthday royalty, she asked us what kind of cake we would like. And each year I would request angel food cake. It seemed exotic. So angel food cake she made me and placed it on that green 10-inch plate I stared at in my hands.

I'm not sure when the tears started. And I'm not sure when they will end, because even now they sneak up on me when I least expect them. But I do know now why my parents held so tightly to the things they had. And why, after they are no longer with us, they will never really be gone.

The green Depression glass plate has a new home. If I'm lucky, it'll be just like the old home — filled with family and friends and laughter. And angel food cake.

— **Paul Kennedy**
Amherst, Wis.

CARNIVAL COLLECTOR CAN'T BELIEVE HIS EYES: TWO RARE BOWLS, ONE DAY
· · · · · · · ·

A few years ago, when I was married, my wife and I set up at an outdoor antiques show in a small village a few miles from home. We had been doing this show twice a year for several years. I liked the show, because it was close to home, and I managed to find some good carnival glass there for my collection.

The Whirling Leaves bowl that sold for $4,400.

After we had her booth set up (my wife was "the dealer" and I was mostly "the help" since I am not a salesperson), I left to walk the show and see if there were any interesting pieces of carnival glass for me. About three quarters of the way through the show, I came upon a table with about six pieces of carnival glass and an elderly gentleman sitting behind it. I picked up a bowl, and while I was looking at it, we struck up a conversation. He told me he came to help his son, who was selling furniture and thought he would try to sell some glass because he had to kill time until they had to leave.

I was inspecting the bowl for any damage when I happened to glance at another bowl sitting on the table. My heart skipped a beat when I saw the color of the glass in its feet. I picked up that bowl and looked at it, trying to not look too excited … let's see … Peacock and Grape … ice cream shape ... spatula footed … and ... lime green opal!

I didn't know what this bowl cost, as there were no prices on his glass but the gentleman soon answered my thoughts. He spoke up and said, "That piece is $35."

That really sent my mind spinning, and with difficult control, I managed to say, "I'll take it." I gave him $35 (no haggling over the price) and rushed the two blocks to my wife. When I showed it to her, her eyes opened wide and she just said, "Oh, my." I told her what I paid for it, and she couldn't believe it. As we were looking at "my find," my thoughts went back to that table and the other glass. The thought sprang into my mind: What color was that bowl that I was looking at first?

I quickly ran back down the street to that table and saw that the other bowl was still sitting there. I approached the table trying to look casual but inside, I was tingling. I picked up the bowl carefully and slowly, held it up to the sky. My stomach started doing flip-flops, and my mind was spinning. I barely heard the gentleman say, "That one is a little more expensive. It is $40."

I thought to myself, "Did he say $40?" Then I heard him say, "I almost bought a book on Millersburg Glass, but it was too expensive."

My mind went back to the bowl in my hands. He was right, this is Millersburg, it is Whirling Leaves, and it is blue; all Millersburg Blue is rare!

To this day I don't know how I kept my voice clear and my hands from shaking when I told him, "I guess I'll take this" and paid him with no haggling.

When I returned to the booth and showed this bowl to my wife, she almost fell out of her chair. "Another one?" she said.

Two spectacular finds in one day and from the same dealer.

I knew the Whirling Leaves bowl was rare, but didn't know just how rare until that night when I checked with an expert in carnival glass. He told me he knew of only two blue Whirling Leaves bowls.

A couple of years later, I placed these two bowls into a carnival glass auction and discovered just how good my finds were that day. The Peacock and Grape Lime Green Opal bowl went for $365 (cost $35) and the Whirling Leaves bowl in blue went for $4,400 (cost $40)!

These were the best two finds out of about eight good pieces of carnival glass I found in that show and village over three or four years. Sad to say, that antiques show ceased to exist a couple of years ago.

— **Don Ruppel**
Saint Charles, Mich.

CARNIVAL GLASS COMPANIES

Here's some helpful information to know when you want to add some carnival glass pieces to your collection:

Much of vintage American carnival glassware was created in the Ohio valley, in the glasshouse-rich areas of Pennsylvania, Ohio and West Virginia. The abundance of natural materials, good transportation and skilled craftsmen that created the early American pattern-glass manufacturing companies allowed many of them to add carnival glass to their production lines. For more information, prices and identification, read "*Warman's Carnival Glass*," 2nd edition, by Ellen Schroy, available at Shop.Collect.com or 800-258-0929.

Brief company histories of the major carnival glass manufacturers follow:

• • • • • • • • •

CAMBRIDGE GLASS COMPANY (CAMBRIDGE)

Cambridge Glass was a rather minor player in the carnival glass marketplace. Founded in 1901 as a new factory in Cambridge, Ohio, it focused on producing fine crystal tablewares. What carnival glass it did produce was imitation cut-glass patterns.

Colors used by Cambridge include marigold, as well as few others. Forms found in carnival glass by Cambridge include tablewares and vases, some with its trademark "Near-Cut."

FENTON ART GLASS COMPANY (FENTON)

Frank Leslie Fenton and his brothers, John W. Fenton and Charles H. Fenton, founded this truly American glassmaker in 1905 in Martins Ferry, Ohio. Frank grew up around glasshouses and started working at one in Indiana, Pa., upon graduating from high school. Within a year, he was foreman at this factory. Three years later, he moved to Jefferson Glass in Steubenville, Ohio, and later to Bastow Glass in Couldersport, Pa. After Bastow Glass burned down, he went to work with Harry Northwood in Wheeling, W. Va. By 1905, he decided his future would be better if he and his brothers went into the glass business for themselves. Early production was of blanks, which the brothers soon learned to decorate themselves. They moved to a larger factory in Williamstown, W. Va.

By 1907, Fenton was experimenting with iridescent glass, developing patterns and the metallic salt formulas for which it became famous. Production of carnival glass continued at Fenton until the early 1930s. In 1970, Fenton began to re-issue carnival glass, creating new colors and forms as well as using traditional patterns. In July 2011, after 106 years of continual production, Fenton announced it would cease production of its collectible and giftware glass products; the glassmaker had faced numerous financial challenges after restructuring in 2007.

Colors developed by Fenton are numerous. The company developed red and Celeste blue in the 1920s; a translucent pale blue, known as Persian blue, is one of its more distinctive colors, as is a light yellow-green color known as vaseline. Fenton also produced delicate opalescent colors, including amethyst and red. Because the Fenton brothers learned how to decorate their own blanks, they also promoted the addition of enamel decoration to some carnival glass patterns.

Fenton made numerous forms. What distinguishes Fenton from other glassmakers is its attention to detail and hand-finishing processes. Edges are found scalloped, fluted, tightly crimped, frilled or pinched into a candy-ribbon edge.

NORTHWOOD GLASS COMPANY (NORTHWOOD)

Englishman Harry Northwood founded the Northwood Glass Company. Like Frank L. Fenton, he, too, was from a glassmaking family, which was well known for making beautiful cameo glass in the Stourbridge area. Also located in that area was the glassmaking facility of Thomas Webb

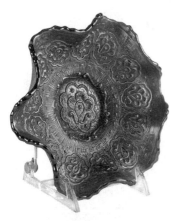

Fenton carnival glass pieces are distinguished by the variety of edges, such as this Persian Medallion sauce with a six-ruffled edge; blue, 6" d.

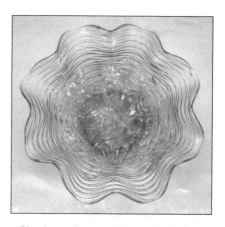

Northwood created its carnival glass in many colors, but its pastels are generally more popular with collectors, such as this Rose Show ruffled bowl in ice blue.

that created "Bronze" and Iris" glass, both iridescent lines. By the time he immigrated to America in 1881, Northwood was influenced by these glassmakers. He became a glass etcher for Hobbs Brockunier Glass Company, Wheeling, W. Va. He moved to La Belle Glass Works, Bridgeport, Ohio, then to Phoenix Glass Co. in Pennsylvania, and back to La Belle. In November 1887, Northwood and other investors bought the old Union Flint Glass factory in Martins Ferry, Ohio, and renamed it Northwood Glass Company. By 1892, the factory was moved to Ellwood City, Pa, but it didn't thrive at this location. In 1895,

Northwood created the new Northwood Glass Company of Indiana, Pa., moving into the former factory of Indiana Glass Company. In 1899, this factory was sold to the new glass conglomerate, National Glass Company. Northwood returned to England as its sales representative, but he must have missed the American glassmakers, because he eventually came back to the States, purchased the old Hobbs Brockunier factory in Wheeling and started the Harry Northwood and Company factory, which continued until 1925. It was at this factory that he developed his glass formulas for carnival glass, naming it "Golden

Iris" in 1908. Northwood was one of the pioneers of the glass manufacturers who marked his wares. Marks range from a full-script signature to a simple underscored capital N in a circle. However, not all Northwood glassware is marked.

Northwood created many colors. Collectors prefer its pastels, such as ice blue, ice green and white. Northwood also is known for several stunning blue shades. The one color that Northwood did not develop was red.

Forms of Northwood patterns range from typical table sets, bowls and water sets. It also produced the to whimsical Corn pattern, which realistically depicts an ear of corn.

MILLERSBURG GLASS COMPANY (MILLERSBURG)

John W. Fenton started the Millersburg Glass Company in September 1908. Perhaps it was the factory's more obscure location or the lack of business experience by John Fenton, but the company failed by 1911.

The factory was bought by Samuel Fair and John Fenton, and renamed the Radium Glass Company, but it lasted only a year.

Millersburg's main forms of carnival glass are bowls and vases. Vintage vase, marigold, 7-1/2".

Colors produced by Millersburg are amethyst, green and marigold. Shades such as blue and vaseline were added on rare occasions. The company is well known for its bright radium finishes. Millersburg produced mostly bowls and vases. Its pattern designers often took one theme and developed several patterns from it, and Millersburg often used one pattern for the interior and a different pattern for the exterior.

DUGAN GLASS COMPANY (DUGAN)

The history of the Dugan Glass

Dugan forms are known for deeply crimped edges. An example is this Apple Blossom Twigs bowl with 3-in-1 edge, purple, 10 ruffles, 9" d.

Company is closely related to Harry Northwood. His cousin, Thomas Dugan, came from the same region in England and grew up around the same glasshouses as Harry Northwood. He immigrated to America in 1881. The cousins worked together at Hobbs Brockunier, Wheeling, W. Va., and also at Northwood Glass Co., Martins Ferry, Ohio. Thomas Dugan became plant manager at the Northwood Glass Co., in Indiana, Pa., in 1895. By 1904, Dugan and his partner, W.G. Minnemayer, bought the former Northwood factory from the now-defunct National Glass conglomerate and opened as the Dugan Glass Company. Dugan's brother, Alfred, joined the company and stayed until it became the Diamond

Glass Company in 1913. At this time, Thomas Dugan moved to the Cambridge Glass Company, later Duncan and Miller and finally Hocking, Lancaster. Alfred left Diamond Glass, too, but later returned.

Understanding how the Northwood and Dugan families were connected helps collectors understand the linkage of these three companies. Their productions were similar; molds were swapped, re-tooled, etc.

Colors attributed to Dugan and Diamond include amethyst, marigold, peach opalescent and white. The company developed deep amethyst shades, some almost black.

Forms made by both Dugan and Diamond mirrored what other glass companies were producing. The significant contribution by Dugan and later Diamond were feet — either ball or spatula shapes. They are also known for deeply crimped edges.

DIAMOND GLASS COMPANY (DIAMOND)

This company was started as the Dugan brothers departed the carnival glass-making scene in 1913. However, Alfred Dugan returned and became general manager until his

Imperial's glass forms tend to be functional, such as this Chatelaine purple water pitcher and tumbler. Water pitcher, 8-1/2" h; tumbler, 4-1/4" h. Both of these pieces are rare.

Although its forms tend to be more functional, US Glass also made whimsies, such as this Palm Beach rose bowl in smoke.

death in 1928. After a disastrous fire in June 1931, the factory closed.

IMPERIAL GLASS COMPANY (IMPERIAL)

Edward Muhleman and a syndicate founded the Imperial Glass Company at Bellaire, Ohio, in 1901, with production beginning in 1904. It started with pressed-glass tableware patterns, as well as lighting fixtures. The company's marketing strategy included selling to important retailers of its day, such as F. W. Woolworth, McCrory and Kresge, to get glassware into the hands of American housewives. Imperial also became a major exporter of glassware, including its brilliant carnival patterns. In 1931, it filed for bankruptcy, but it was able to continue. By 1962, it was again producing carnival glass. The factory was closed in 1985 and the molds sold.

Colors made by Imperial include typical carnival colors, such as marigold. It added interesting shades of green, known as helios, a pale ginger-ale shade known as clambroth, and a brownish smoke shade. Imperial's forms tend to be functional, such as berry sets and table sets. Patterns vary from wonderful imitation cut-glass patterns to detailed florals and naturalistic designs.

UNITED STATES GLASS COMPANY (US GLASS)

In 1891, a consortium of 15 Ameri-

An example of Westmoreland's work is this Corinth jack-in-the-pulpit vase in blue opalescent, 9-1/2" h.

can glass manufacturers formed the United States Glass Company, which was successful in continuing pattern-glass production as well as developing new glass lines. By 1911, it had begun limited production of carnival glass lines, often using existing pattern-glass tableware molds. By the time a tornado destroyed the last of its glass factories in Glassport in 1963, it was no longer producing glassware.

Colors associated with US Glass are marigold, white and a rich honey amber. Its forms tend to be table sets and other functional pieces.

WESTMORELAND GLASS COMPANY (WESTMORELAND)

Started in 1889 as the Westmore-land Speciality Company in Grapeville, Pa., this company originally made novelties and glass packing containers, such as candy containers.

Researchers have identified its patterns being advertised by Butler Brothers as early as 1908. Carnival glass production continued into the 1920s. In the 1970s, Westmoreland, too, begin to re-issue carnival glass patterns and novelties. However, this ceased in February 1996 when the factory burned.

Colors originally used by Westmoreland were typical carnival colors, such as blue and marigold. Forms include tableware, containers and other functional forms.

TIME LINE

1889 Westmoreland Specialty Glass Company founded in Grapeville, Pa.

1901 Cambridge Glass is founded in Cambridge, Ohio.

1904 Dugan Glass Company forms.

1904 Glass production begins at Imperial Glass.

1905 Fenton Glass Company founded in Martins Ferry, Ohio

1907 Documentation exists showing Fenton experimenting with metallic salts to create iridescent colors.

1908 Harry Northwood develops Golden Iris.

1908 John W. Fenton founds Millersburg Glass Company.

1908 Butler Brothers first advertise a "Golden Sunset Iridescent Assortment" of glassware. This assortment was made by Fenton and included its Beaded Star, Diamond Point Columns and Waterlily and Cattails patterns.

1910 Butler Brothers advertises Westmoreland patterns such as Scales, Louisa and Smooth Rays as an "Antique Iridescent Novelty Assortment."

1911 Imperial advertises its Imperial Grape line in Amber Flame, Dragon Blue, Helios and Azure.

1911 Butler Brothers advertise Millersburg patterns such as Rose Columns, Peacock at Urn, Dolphin and Cherries.

1911 Millersburg Glass Company files for bankruptcy.

1911 Millersburg factory changes hands and becomes Radium Glass Co.

1911 US Glass starts production of carnival glass.

1912 Radium Glass Company goes out of business.

1912 Butler Brothers advertises US Glass patterns, including Palm Beach and Cosmos & Cane.

1913 Dugan Glass Company closes.

1913 Diamond Glass Company forms.

1915 Imperial advertises patterns such as Lustre Rose, Imperial Grape, Pansy, Double Dutch, Ripple and Windmill.

1915 Diamond advertises patterns such as Stork and Rushes, Vining Twigs, Beaded Basket, Maple Leaf, Persian Garden, Leaf Rays and Windflower.

1919 Harry Northwood dies.

1920s Fenton introduces red and celeste blue.

1920 Westmoreland discontinues carnival glass production.

1925 Harry Northwood and Company goes out of business.

1930s Fenton switches its focus from carnival glass to other glasswares.

1931 Diamond Glass Company closes.

1948 Frank L. Fenton dies.

1950s Imperial buys out Cambridge Glass.

1962 Imperial begins to re-make carnival glass.

1963 US Glass closes.

1970 Fenton re-issues carnival glass.

1970s Westmoreland re-issues carnival glass.

1985 Imperial Glass closes.

1996 Westmoreland closes.

COLORS OF CARNIVAL GLASS

In carnival glass, think of "color, color, color" as real estate agents do "location, location, location." Color is certainly what carnival glass is all about. There are two types of colors that carnival glass collectors need to know.

The first is the base color. To determine the base color of carnival glass, you need to find the marie (non-iridized base). The next step is to hold the piece up to check the color. Having a strong light source is crucial to determining the base color, as knowing the base color will help you determine the value of your carnival glass.

While still holding the piece near that strong light source, examine the iridescent coloration to determine the color of that as well as the base color. Knowing the pattern is the third most important element in determining value.

Carnival glass collectors now recognize more than 60 colors of glassware. It is important to remember that every glass manufacturer had its own recipes for batch colors and also secret combinations of the metallic salts that created the iridescent effect. Add to that the thought that every one of us perceives color slightly different, and you can easily see how variations exist and that no two pieces of carnival glass are the same. Embracing these variations helps collectors find the treasured pieces of carnival glass and enjoy them for years.

Listed here are brief explanations of the colors seen most often.

• • • • • • • • •

AMBER, HONEY AMBER

Amber is a yellow to brown tinted base glass, which usually shows off multicolored iridescence well. Honey amber is a brownish-marigold iridescence on a clear base. This color is usually restricted to US Glass pieces.

AMBERINA

Amberina is a blend of red glass shading to a yellowish color. Putting selenium into the molten batch causes the red coloration. When the mixture is reheated, the colors blend into amberina.

AMETHYST, LAVENDER AND PURPLE

The terms amethyst, lavender and purple were used interchangeably for many years of carnival glass collecting. Today, collectors prefer to identify pieces as amethyst when the base color of a piece is a medium to light shade of purple; lavender pieces as the lightest shade of purple; and purple when they resemble deep purple grape juice.

AQUA, AQUA OPALESCENT

Aqua carnival glass is a pretty shade of light blue with a hint of green. Some collectors call pieces "teal" when the blue is more dominant.

Aqua opalescent is popular with carnival glass collectors, as it combines the vibrancy of aqua with the allure of milky-white opalescence and marigold carnival iridescence. Northwood perfected the color and created most of the known aqua opalescent pieces.

Butterscotch refers to the color created when marigold iridescence is found on an aqua opalescent base.

BLACK AMETHYST

Black amethyst is such a dense color that it appears almost opaque. It is the name used to describe a very deep amethyst.

BLUES: CELESTE, ICE, PERSIAN, POWDER, RENNINGER AND SAPPHIRE

Generally when blue is used to describe the base color of a piece, it is cobalt blue, but there are many colors and variations.

Celeste blue is created when pastel iridescence is used over a blue base. Ice blue is a base color that is a very pale blue; Northwood introduced its ice blue in 1912.

Persian blue is a light blue base with a pastel iridescent finish. Most pieces in this color exhibit a cloudy appearance.

Powder blue is a medium-blue opaque, often called slag glass by collectors.

Renninger blue is created when a dark marigold iridescence is used over a dark blue to purple base, with some turquoise influence. Its name was coined after so many examples of this shade were found at Renninger's Flea Markets.

Sapphire blue is created when marigold iridescence is used over a blue base.

CLAMBROTH

Clambroth is a color that is determined by the iridescence. The coloration is a light marigold over a slightly tinted base. Some collectors call pieces with a weak iridescence on a clear base clambroth. Imperial was responsible for most of the lightly tinted bases associated with this color. One of its most popular colors is known as "Ginger Ale" because of the close similarity to beverage color.

GREENS: GREEN, EMERALD GREEN, HELIOS, ICE GREEN, LIME GREEN, LIME GREEN OPALESCENT, OLIVE GREEN AND RUSSET GREEN

As with many carnival colors, every manufacturer's recipe for green was slightly different. Fenton's green tends to be intense, while Millersburg's is lighter. Emerald green carnival glass is a deep, rich green; both Imperial and Northwood made emerald green. Helios is Imperial's original name for its interesting shade of green that is found with a pale golden iridescence. Ice green is a pale green base color covered with a frosty-looking pastel iridescence; Northwood introduced its ice green in 1912. Lime green is a bright, almost-neon green; it can be found with marigold iridescence. Lime green opalescent is a lime-green base with pastel iridescence.

Olive green is a deep, brownish green, usually found with a marigold iridescent finish. Russet is an olive- to brown-toned green.

HOREHOUND

Horehound is a smoky gray base color, usually with blue or green highlights. It can also be a brownish tone.

MARIGOLD, MARIGOLD OVER MILK GLASS, PASTEL MARIGOLD AND PUMPKIN MARIGOLD

The most predominant color in carnival glass is marigold. It is the only color that takes its coloration from the iridescent treatment, because it is usually on a clear glass body. If you think of marigold flowers, this color will be easy to remember, as it is often a vibrant orange-toned hue.

Marigold over milk glass is a combination that blends a bright marigold iridescence with a slightly translucent white milk-glass base. Sometimes this is also called Moonstone. Pastel marigold is marigold iridescence over a clear glass body, but the iridescent finish is reheated into a satin finish, creating a soft color, often more yellow tone than the bright orange associated with marigold.

Pumpkin marigold is a collector's name for a deep, dark marigold shade, more reminiscent of pumpkins than a marigold blossom.

PEACH OPALESCENT

Peach opalescent is a color that varies with each piece, as the opalescence was created by reheating. Bone ash is added to the glass to create this milky-white effect as the piece cooled. Dugan perfected the process and made the greatest quantity of this color. In addition to the milky-white opalescent areas, the pieces will usually have a marigold iridescence.

RED

Red is one of the most sought-after carnival base colors. The red coloration is caused by putting selenium into the molten batch. Fenton and Imperial both created strong reds.

REVERSE AMBERINA

Reverse amberina occurs when a piece shades from a red base to a yellow rim. The red coloration is caused by putting selenium into the molten batch. When the mixture is reheated, the colors blend into amberina.

SMOKE

Smoke is a light gray base with iridescence that usually includes an iridescent cast of colors as blue, green, amber or brown. Imperial and Northwood made smoke-colored pieces.

VASELINE

The base color for vaseline is a light green-yellow. Because of uranium oxide added to create this color, it will glow if subjected to black light.

WHITE

White is another color found on a clear base. The coloration is derived from a pastel iridescent finish. Dugan, Fenton, Millersburg and Northwood all made white forms, each one differing slightly in hue. Northwood introduced its icy white in 1912.

WISTERIA

Wisteria is a light, delicate amethyst base color.

DEPRESSION GLASS
IDENTIFICATION GUIDE

Depression-era glassware can be confusing. Many times, one manufacturer came up with a neat new design, and as soon as it was successful, other companies started to make patterns that were similar. To help you figure out what pattern you might be trying to research, here's a quick identification guide. The patterns are broken down into several different classifications by design elements. Try comparing your piece to these. For more information, prices and identification, read *Warman's Depression Glass*, 5th edition, by Ellen Schroy, available at Shop.Collect.com or 800-258-0929.

• • • • • • • • •

ART DECO

Ovide

BASKETS

Lorain

BEADED EDGES

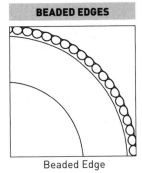

Beaded Edge

BEADED EDGES

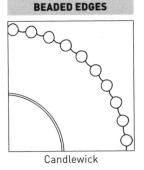

Candlewick

BIRDS

Delilah

Georgian

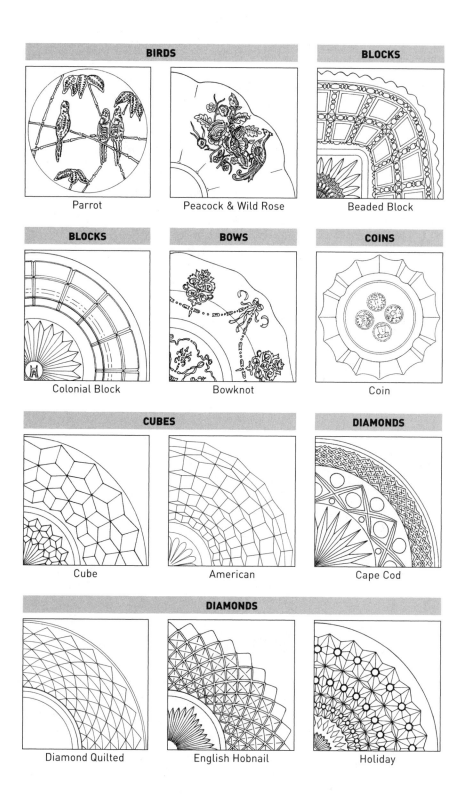

BIRDS

Parrot

Peacock & Wild Rose

BLOCKS

Beaded Block

BLOCKS

Colonial Block

BOWS

Bowknot

COINS

Coin

CUBES

Cube

American

DIAMONDS

Cape Cod

DIAMONDS

Diamond Quilted

English Hobnail

Holiday

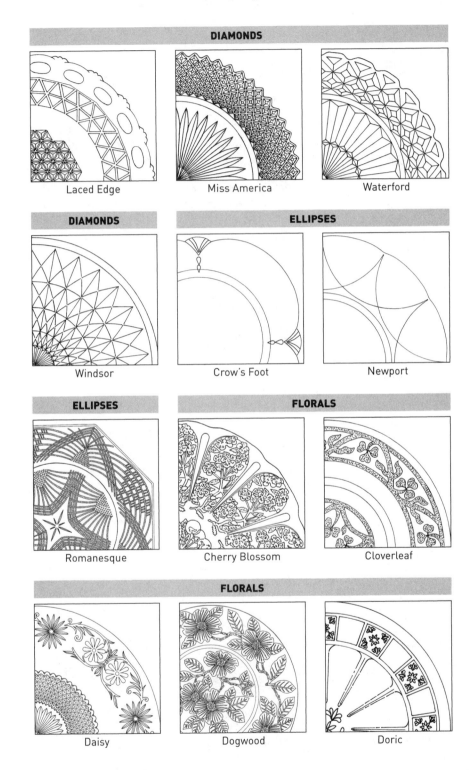

DIAMONDS

Laced Edge

Miss America

Waterford

DIAMONDS

Windsor

ELLIPSES

Crow's Foot

Newport

ELLIPSES

Romanesque

FLORALS

Cherry Blossom

Cloverleaf

FLORALS

Daisy

Dogwood

Doric

Doric & Pansy

Floragold

Floral

Floral and Diamond Band

Flower Garden
with Butterflies

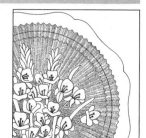
Iris

Jubilee

Mayfair

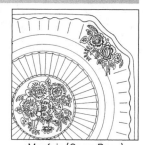
Mayfair (Open Rose)

Normandie

Pineapple & Floral

Rose Cameo

CHAPTER 3 — GLASS

FLORALS

Rosemary

Royal Lace

Sharon

FLORALS

Sunflower

Thistle

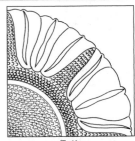

Tulip

FIGURES

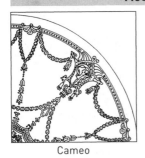

Cameo

Cupid

FRUITS

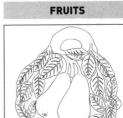

Avocado

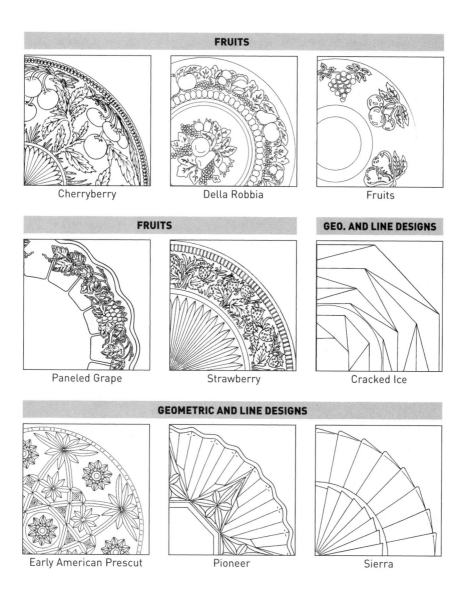

FRUITS

Cherryberry

Della Robbia

Fruits

FRUITS

GEO. AND LINE DESIGNS

Paneled Grape

Strawberry

Cracked Ice

GEOMETRIC AND LINE DESIGNS

Early American Prescut

Pioneer

Sierra

GEOMETRIC AND LINE DESIGNS

Starlight

Tea Room

HONEYCOMB

Hex Optic

HONEYCOMB

Aunt Polly

HORSESHOE

Horseshoe

LACY DESIGNS

Heritage

LACY DESIGNS

S-Pattern

Sandwich (Line 41)

Sandwich (Hocking)

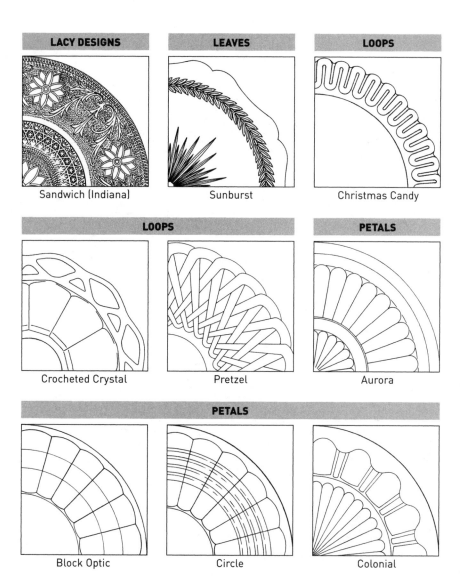

LACY DESIGNS

Sandwich (Indiana)

LEAVES

Sunburst

LOOPS

Christmas Candy

LOOPS

Crocheted Crystal

Pretzel

PETALS

Aurora

PETALS

Block Optic

Circle

Colonial

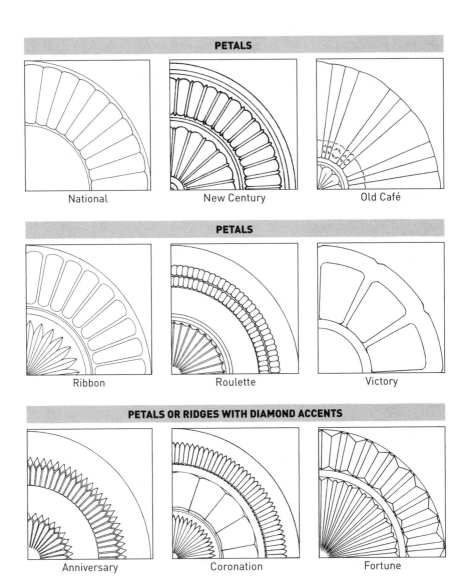

PETALS

National

New Century

Old Café

PETALS

Ribbon

Roulette

Victory

PETALS OR RIDGES WITH DIAMOND ACCENTS

Anniversary

Coronation

Fortune

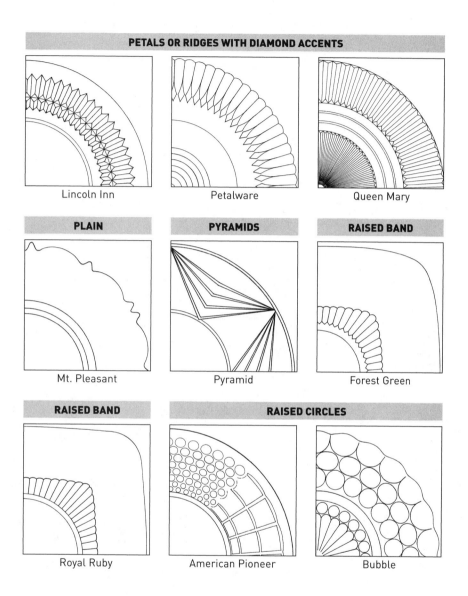

PETALS OR RIDGES WITH DIAMOND ACCENTS

Lincoln Inn

Petalware

Queen Mary

PLAIN

Mt. Pleasant

PYRAMIDS

Pyramid

RAISED BAND

Forest Green

RAISED BAND

Royal Ruby

RAISED CIRCLES

American Pioneer

Bubble

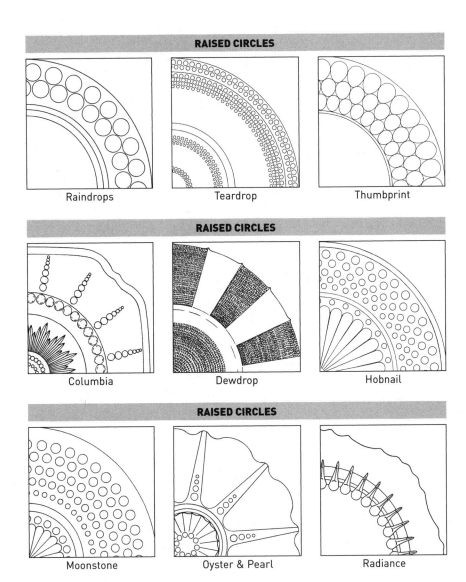

Raindrops

Teardrop

Thumbprint

RAISED CIRCLES

Columbia

Dewdrop

Hobnail

RAISED CIRCLES

Moonstone

Oyster & Pearl

Radiance

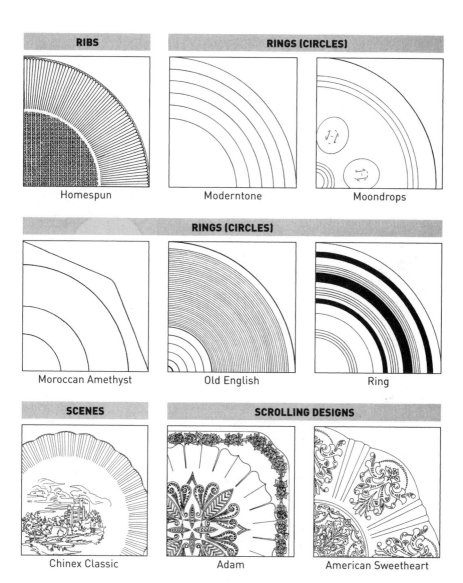

RIBS

Homespun

RINGS (CIRCLES)

Moderntone

Moondrops

RINGS (CIRCLES)

Moroccan Amethyst

Old English

Ring

SCENES

Chinex Classic

SCROLLING DESIGNS

Adam

American Sweetheart

Florentine No. 1

Florentine No. 2

Madrid

Patrick

Princess

Rock Crystal

Roxana

Vernon

Colony

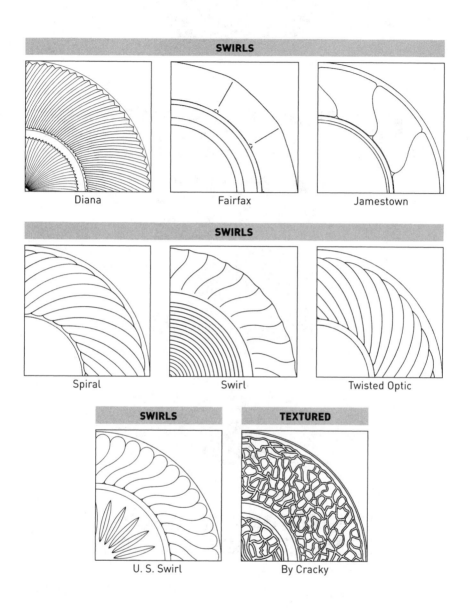

SWIRLS

Diana   Fairfax   Jamestown

SWIRLS

Spiral   Swirl   Twisted Optic

SWIRLS   **TEXTURED**

U. S. Swirl   By Cracky

CHAPTER 4

DECORATIVE ARTS

COLLECTOR GETS SECOND CHANCE TO SEE THE LIGHT

· · · · · · · · ·

Who hasn't passed over a desirable antique because it seemed too expensive, only to be "haunted" by it later on? I have a friend who says such items often "speak" to her. If they speak loud enough or long enough, she returns to purchase them. I have experienced that exact same nagging situation many times throughout my collecting career.

Sometimes, after much deliberation, I return to buy the item — I just have to have it! Other times, I just let it go. Once, I saved up three times to purchase a set of leaded-glass windows. Each time, the money was diverted to some emergency: The water heater gave out, the cat broke my glasses, tax rates rose. Eventually, I found the money and made the elusive acquisition.

One of my most unusual "hauntings" occurred a few years ago. Intrigued by an ad in the local penny saver, I trudged over hill and dale to a house located miles down a country road and deep in the woods. "House full of antiques for sale" the ad read, or something to that effect ... and boy was it! The house was a modern log cabin, and every nook and cranny was loaded with antiques and collectibles.

Unfortunately, there were no bargains, but I did spy an interesting Bradley and Hubbard floor lamp with ornate brass table-like shelves. It was topped with the most extraordinary etched cranberry glass shade. I almost missed it, obscured among all the surrounding ephemera. In my 35-plus years of antiquing, I had never seen anything like it. However, it was too costly for my budget at that time, so I left empty handed.

Months went by, and I thought about it once in a while. The lamp "spoke" to me rather faintly from time to time. Had they sold it? Should I go back? I never did. A year or so later, I found myself attending an auction in another town about 45 minutes away. During the preview, I noticed a brass lamp stand identical to the one I had passed up, except it had no shade. I told the auctioneer my story and mentioned that the lamp I had previously seen was crowned by a beautiful cranberry glass shade. The auctioneer reached into a nearby box, pulled out a shade, and asked, "Did it look like this?"

To my gob-struck surprise, it was the very same lamp, consigned by the people from the log cabin! There was no more thinking and wondering. If I wanted it, now was my second chance. I am happy to report that after taxes and the buyer's premium, I saved a whole whopping $67.

— **J.C. Russell**
Upstate New York

GRANDMA'S 'MODIFIED' CHAIRS HOLD SPECIAL MEANING

• • • • • • • •

One of my favorite finds, although not valuable to most, is a special treasure to me! My mom had given me two wooden dining chairs that she had gotten from her parents' estate. Originally, there were eight matching chairs that had belonged to my Grandpa and his brother.

When my grandpa decided to marry (he married my grandma in 1898 and together they had 11 children), he and his brother each took four of these chairs. After my grandparents set up their household, my grandmother got frustrated when she dusted these chairs. She said the spindles were too close together in the back to dust sufficiently, so she sawed out three of the seven spindles out of the backs of her four chairs.

In 2008, at my mom's sister's sale, lo and behold, there was one of grandma and grandpa's chairs that matched mine with three missing spindles! So I purchased the chair, and I'm waiting for a fourth chair to surface that is missing three of its spindles. I am continuing to watch at local auctions in the hopes of finding the fourth matching chair that will complete my treasure! I smile each time I dust in between the spindles and think of my grandmother, who I never had the pleasure of knowing in this world.

My chairs continue to seat my family and guests around our table and still hold a special place in my heart.

— **Bonnie Rebel**
Ness City, Kan.

ARMOIRE HAS PLACE OF PRIDE

· · · · · · · · ·

I think my greatest rummage sale/yard sale find was a mahogany armoire I was lucky enough to find about eight years ago.

I stopped at a yard sale in White Springs, Fla. The yard had table after table of glass and ceramic items. The folks running the sale told me their children were saving up to go to Wild Adventures, a theme park in Valdosta, Ga. I happen to be from Valdosta, so I knew exactly what they were excited about. The family was having the yard sale to help the kids raise the money.

They showed me an old armoire that had come out of the old house they lived in. The residence appeared to have been built in the 1920s or '30s. The armoire was covered in white paint, the thickest white paint you can imagine and some-one had played a dart game using the doors as the targets.

The doors had carved clusters of grapes peering out from under the clumps of white paint. I looked inside and could see the original wood. I believed it to be mahogany. I could see possibilities here!

My mind was churning, and I was getting more excited by the minute. I asked what was the least they would take for it. They said $250. I told them I was go-ing to have to spend several hundred dollars to get it in shape. They finally said $200. I turned around to walk away and the man said $175 was the least he could take.

I wanted to get the price down, but I also wanted the kids to go to Wild Adven-tures, so I agreed. I backed the truck up to the long front porch and it took me, my son, and the man and his wife working diligently to get the armoire loaded. There were two parts: a top section with doors and bottom drawers, and a lower section, which served as a stand or cradle.

To make a long story short, I was able to get it back home and had it restored to the original wood. It is Honduras mahogany, according to the restorer, and is one of my most prized possessions.

— **Connie M. Williams**
Valdosta, Ga.

THRIFT STORE 'COFFEE POT' IS EARLY AMERICAN PEWTER

• • • • • • • • •

My find happened on a sunny July morning. I awoke and said, "I need to relax." And the only way to really relax is to do my thing at the thrift store.

The local thrift stores in my area are always full of people, and they play that good soul music. Everyone is in a good mood and seems to stay longer when the beat is really good.

On this day, they were playing "Surfin' Bird" with the "pa-pa-ooma-mow-mow, papa-ooma-mow-mow," and I even saw a grandma step to the beat. Once I recovered I began to look with interest along the wall where the glass and metal objects were placed.

I first scanned along the wall to see if there was anything of interest. I saw something that caught my eye because it was so distinguishable from the other items. I immediately wanted to see it up close, but in my heart I knew that this was the one. I knew the item was special.

The thrift stores in California carry such a diverse array of items that it's difficult to find one particular item you just have to have. But this item was classic — the lines, the design, the beauty was indescribable. I had to have it: a pewter coffee pot.

The classically designed acorn-shape pot has a wooden handle, which is what caught my eye. I have several tea and water carafes with wooden handles, and this was the opportunity for me to add to my collection.

Little did I know the significance of the find. First, I thought it was a teapot, but after I brought it home and started to research the item, the facts didn't fit that assumption, so I started with the facts that I had.

The maker's mark began my journey. When I looked at the maker, there were the words, "Wallace Bros. Silversmiths PV19 PEWTER." My first search led me to a website about silversmiths and related craftsman. Voila! I found the right website to give me the information about the Wallace Bros., but it didn't explain the size and shape of the teapot.

A different website explained the various shapes and sizes from the different periods coffee pots and teapots were manufactured. That is where I saw the shape of my pot and learned it was not a teapot, but rather a coffeepot.

I was thrilled to find my item and learned there were very few real pewter coffeepots in existence made in America that have survived. Although it looked like a coffeepot I saw in an illustration, I needed to confirm it with experts. I knew of Colonial Williamsburg from Queen Elizabeth's visit and the Winterthur Museum. But I was scared to contact them with what may have been a foolish assumption. But I did, and I am very happy and proud to say my pewter coffee pot was confirmed as such by a curator, and that made my day.

I am now in the process of researching two other marks on the pot with the Connecticut Historical Society for their significance if any to the provenance of the coffee pot.

— **S. Denise Smith**
via e-mail

SOUTHWEST DANCER FINDS A GOOD NEW ENGLAND HOME

· · · · · · · · ·

The year was 1972. The place was a graduate school dorm at the University of Arizona in Tucson. Not in my wildest dreams did I imagine that by grumpily answering a wrong number from a phone that rang 37 times outside my dorm room, at 3:15 a.m., during finals week, my life would start a new chapter. Why? I ended up marrying that wrong number!

Within a few years, my husband and I knew that jobs were taking us away from Tucson, so we started collecting the arts of the Southwest that we loved: a Navajo dye chart, sand paintings, woven rugs, Papago baskets (as they were referred to then), Zuni and Hopi inlaid turquoise and silver jewelry and a beaded papoose carrier purchased from a trading post.

After a two-year building project in Florida, 1980 found us happily settled in Meredith, N.H., looking forward to raising our daughters in a small-town setting. We took on civic duties, and as a teacher turned stay-at-home mom, my interests were in school activities. I soon became the fundraising chairwoman for our newly formed Parent Teacher Organization, and one of our first activities was an all-school yard sale.

Stuff came in from everywhere. Loads and loads of stuff filled the elementary school as well as the parking lot. While working a volunteer shift, one of the parents who was also helping out joked: "Karen, don't you absolutely need that cute little Indian dancer for your house?"

At the time she, had no idea that my entire downstairs was decorated with our Southwest treasures. I followed her gaze, looking on the ground and saw, propped up by a table leg, a perfect, signed, Navajo sand painting, similar to the ones in our collection. The price was 25 cents.

As it turned out, I did absolutely need that Yei bi Chai dancer by Marie Billie. I quickly put down my quarter, not knowing who donated the sand painting or what the circumstances were but clearly understanding the old adage: "One man's trash is another man's treasure."

To this day, despite all of the lovely old New England antiques with which we continue to furnish our home, the sand painting is one of my favorite finds. Although we don't get back to Tucson very often, our Southwest collections still lovingly dominate our family room!

— **Karen Sticht**
Meredith, N.H.

NAVAJO RUG SNAGGED FOR $5

· · · · · · · · ·

A few years back, I went to garage sales looking for new treasures. One place I went was an old lumber store an older gentleman had converted to be his home. He was going to move and was selling most of his belongings.

It was pretty crowded, but I noticed everyone was walking on a particular rug. It was very faded, but when I had a chance, I picked up one end to see the reverse side. I don't believe it had ever been turned over as long as it had been there. I asked him if he would sell it, and he said $5. Sounded good to me, so up it came and out I went.

It was an old Navajo rug, but unusually large. It measured about 96 inches by 72 inches. The back side was tan with a black and red design. The colors were still quite bright compared to the other side. There were a couple small wear holes, but not too bad.

I took pictures and sent them to an appraiser in Santa Fe, N.M., and was very pleased with the results. He appraised it for $800 retail and $400 wholesale. I kept it for a while and sold it to a dealer for $250: A pretty good return for my $5.

— **Heidi Phelps**
via e-mail

LOUISIANA ART REDISCOVERED IN CALIFORNIA

· · · · · · · · ·

About 15 years ago, my husband and I attended the Ventura County Flea Market in Ventura, Calif. We split up, looking for items, when I spotted a wonderful oil painting of a Louisiana swamp scene. It was a painting of a sunset and depicted a seafood processing drop-off dock, where the workers were unloading the day's catch from the fishing and shrimp boats.

In the painting were the shrimp boats coming in and the workers taking the catch into a large shed. In the forefront was a black man under the trees, fishing with a cane pole with a whiskey jug next to him.

It was titled "Swamp Idyll" and signed Colette Pope Heldner. Since my husband is a Louisiana Cajun who put himself through Louisiana State University working on oil rigs and shrimp boats, I purchased the painting for $18 to surprise him. The oil painting measured 16 inches by 30 inches framed and was in excellent condition. I thought: "I'm going to buy it. What can I lose?"

We have since learned that Colette Pope Heldner is a famous Southern Impressionist, and her works have sold for thousands! My husband loves the painting, and we would not part with it because it is part of who we are. Whoever thought I would find this wonderful painting at a flea market in California? You never know.

— **Georgia Dupuis**
via e-mail

DAD'S $300 FLATWARE FIND CREATES A MONSTER

· · · · · · · · ·

From the mid-1970s through the '80s, garage-sale shopping was a necessity for stretching my meager teaching salary. Garage, or "yard sales" as we call them here, helped with household needs as well as with unprovided classroom essentials ranging from library books to craft materials.

My father teased me about my purchases at first, but began to notice some of the "good stuff" I came home with. Soon he began visiting yard sales upon occasion.

The "yard sale bug" bit him badly the day he found six sterling silver forks wrapped up with a piece of masking tape, marked with a price of $1.

"Uh, is this $1 each, or for the bundle?" Dad asked, swallowing hard in amazement, regardless of what the answer would be. He was assured the price was for the bundle and said, "I'll take them!"

Before coming home that day, Dad stopped at the local jewelry store and asked questions. The pattern was still current and pictured in a catalog.

It was difficult to tell from a small picture, and lacking something to compare, but depending upon whether these were salad or dinner forks, the price was either $52 or $58 apiece! With more than a 300 percent return on that $1 investment, Dad became a yard sale regular!

Now it falls to me to wisely dispose of all those accumulated "treasures!" Anybody need sterling silver forks, cameras, vases, knives, bird feeders, clocks or ... ?

— **Karla Gilbert**
Montrose, Colo.

THIS FAVORITE FIND
WAS AN IMPULSE PURCHASE
· · · · · · · · ·

My favorite find was an impulse purchase, pure and simple.

I was at an estate auction in the spring of 2010. I don't think I was even there for anything specific, when a green painted blanket chest came up for bid. I hadn't seen it during the auction preview, so my first glimpse of it was from the middle of the crowd, half a room away. But I did notice that it would match the hutch in my dining room perfectly, and I was smitten with its form and slightly weathered charm. I craned my neck and tried to get a better look, but couldn't quite see it all.

As I recall, bidding was slow to start. I made a quick decision and decided to "go for it" — I didn't want this to be one of those items that I let get away. I'm always on the lookout for new (or old, in this case) storage solutions. I jumped in and bid. I couldn't believe it when bidding closed at just $10!

You may wonder why I would want a blanket chest in my dining room, but I'm all for re-purposing pieces regardless of their original use. At the moment, I'm using it to store games and puzzles, and it comes in handy for extra seating when I have large family gatherings.

When I think about what makes this blanket chest my personal favorite find,

I have to say it's because I've never had an iota of regret from buying it. I get pleasure seeing it each day, and I'm happy because the storage it provides gives it a purpose.

I don't think the low price has much to do with it being my favorite find since

I've bought things for considerably less at auctions and yard sales and regretted buying them. I admit it was a lucky buy: It didn't have any condition issues, and when I got it home, it really did match my hutch. In any case, I don't recommend buying at auction without thoroughly inspecting the merchandise!

It's been more than a year since I've bought my charming little blanket chest, and I suspect it will be my favorite find for some time to come. But that doesn't mean I won't be looking for more pieces to keep it company.

— **Karen Knapstein,**
Iola, Wis.

MYSTICAL STAINED GLASS APPRAISED FOR THOUSANDS

· · · · · · · ·

About eight years ago, I visited an estate sale in my neighborhood. The sale was in the basement of the house, and everything was quite dark. The owners had passed on, and the relatives were selling off contents of the house.

After selecting a few household items, I came across a small piece of stained

glass that measured 10 inches by 10 inches. The stained glass was dated in the 1500s and had a coat of arms and devil design and had armor, mystical fish, shields, lions, etc.

Thinking the date in the 1500s could not be correct, I put it down and walked away. But what if I was wrong? I went back a few times before asking the 15-year-old boy who was helping his mother sell off the things how much they wanted for the stained glass. He took it from me, held it up the light and said, "You mean this thing with the foreign writing on it? We want $10 for it."

He was holding it backwards and the date from the 1500s was being read backwards! I decided to take a chance and purchased this item. Although I have never formally had this appraised in person, I sent a photo to the Philadelphia Museum of Art, and they told me it was likely an old piece of Swiss stained glass that perhaps was once owned by the museum itself before [the staff] cleared out a collection in the early 20th century.

A work colleague of mine whose brother worked for Sotheby's told him he would appraise it for about $5,000.

— **Phil Hasegawa**
via e-mail

RARE TREASURE FOUND ... FOR SOMEONE ELSE

· · · · · · · · ·

My greatest find wasn't even for me.

In the 1990s, I got a call from a fellow — let's call him Tom — inquiring about some John Harvard bookends. A set had recently sold online, and since I am a bookend collector, Tom thought I might be able to help him find another set. I subsequently learned that he is a collector of all things Harvard-related. As commonly happens amongst collectors, the following conversation unfolded:

Me: So what is the 'holy grail' amongst Harvard collectors?

Tom: Well, you know the figures in those bookends? There's actually an individual bronze sculpture, signed by the sculptor Daniel Chester French, of which only a couple dozen were made, that look just like the bookends. There's one in the library at Harvard. It was made by the Griffoul Foundry of Newark, N.J.

Me: OK. If I see one, you'll be the first to know (like I might EVER).

Fast forward six months. I am at Brimfield, 1998, walking a field, when I spot ... could it be? A bronze statue that reads "Griffoul," DC French. I quickly dial the phone.

Me: Hi. I don't know if you remember me, but I think I found something you're interested in...

Tom: Describe it for me.

Me: (thorough description)

Tom: THAT'S IT!

Me: Hold on a second.

I negotiate with the dealer to put down a deposit on the bronze. Tom and the dealer work out the fine details of full payment over the phone. A week later, I get an excited call from Tom. He informs me that this is indeed the great rarity he has been looking for.

Finding a treasure can be just as exciting when you find something that is a jewel for someone else. This acquisition was not a monetary success: I did not charge Tom anything for finding this item, but merely linked a seller and a buyer. The small cash deposit I had left ($200) was perhaps a risk. But after my original conversation with Tom on the phone, learning about his collecting interests, his current travails as a graduate student and his family's history at Harvard, I had confidence that he was a "solid citizen."

Tom promptly returned the deposit I had placed for him. According to its appraisal, this particular item is the most valuable item I have ever been involved in acquiring, though I never owned it myself. It's always been kind of amazing that a chance conversation, followed by a chance find, can coincide so well to result in a rare treasure being brought home to appreciative treasure collector.

— **Louis Kuritzky**
Gainesville, Fla.

CHINA CABINET: $30
KARMA: TO BE DETERMINED
• • • • • • • •

In the early 1980s, my oldest daughter and grandson came over to visit and go garage-sale shopping. Stopping first in my neighborhood at a moving sale, the man holding the sale asked what we were looking for. I said I was looking for something to put my books in. He showed me a china cabinet in the bedroom, adding that this should be the thing for my books.

I asked how much, and he said $30. I said I would take it, but since I had no way to get it home, he held it for me since I live two streets over from him. I gave him $20, my phone number and my name, and said when my husband came home from work we would pick it up.

That's what I did when my husband came home. I wouldn't let him out of his truck. "We have to go pick up my china cabinet," I told him.

I paid the $10, and we loaded the cabinet and brought it home.

That night, the man called me and said I cheated him. I told him I asked the price, and he told me the price. I paid what he asked. He said his girlfriend came home and said he could have gotten more. I said, "I paid what you asked."

Later, I heard he and his wife were divorcing, and while she was out of town, the husband and his girlfriend were selling everything out of the house!

— **Martha Boles**
Altamonte Springs, Fla.

P.S. [The cabinet] is filled not only with books but with dolls, tea sets and so much more.

$15 YARD-SALE GAMBLE IS A $600 EBAY SCORE

•••••••••

In 2007, I flew from Las Vegas to White Plains, N.Y. I arrived in the morning, and my daughter patiently took me yard saling on the way to her home in Connecticut.

At one of the stops, I found a set of vintage Dansk stainless steel flatware for $15. I paid the $15 with concerns I might not recoup my investment. As it turned out, the pattern was "Thistle," highly desired and retired. The set, with a starting bid of $19.98, sold for more than $600 on eBay. That remains my favorite yard sale find, and I love Dansk!

— **Patricia Gerstenmaier**
Las Vegas, Nev.

POSSIBLE LYON WATERCOLOR HIDDEN IN BOY SCOUT SALE

•••••••••

At a Boy Scout fundraiser, I bought a watercolor, and on the back was a small white sticker that said: Watercolor by Lyon. There is no signature on the watercolor, therefore I'm just going by what the little white sticker said.

The watercolor was laid down on a piece of cardboard and marked off in pencil so it could fit into the frame. The size of the watercolor is 11 inches by 21 inches. I did some research, and I believe that this might have been done by George Francis Lyon when he was commissioned by The British Government to go on an expedition into the interior of Africa to find the Niger River. This would have been around 1818. The watercolor resembles what the coastline of the island of Malta or Tripoli might have looked like at the beginning of the 1800s, when George Lyon was stationed on the island of Malta.

I sent photos to an appraisal site called "What is it Worth to You," and they told me that it did resemble other watercolors done by George Lyon.

I wish that I had taken it to an "Antiques Roadshow" stop in Pittsburgh, because they might have been able to give me more information on its value and if it was actually done by George Lyon.

— **Thomas Allshouse**
East Brady, Pa.

A $2 TIFFANY LAMP
LANDS OWNER ON TV
· · · · · · · · ·

My favorite find was my $2 Tiffany lamp. It was a rarely found, small, all-bronze Tiffany I found at an even smaller backyard estate sale.

This was in the early 1990s, and our son was on the Brother Martin High School football team in New Orleans, La. I noticed the sale on Elysian Fields Avenue on our way to practice one Saturday morning. I couldn't wait for practice to end, so I left my son to his father for his ride home. I headed straight to the sale.

At first I was somewhat disappointed. The grandkids said that their grandma had worked for many families in uptown New Orleans during her life, and they had always passed on things to her when they redecorated or simply got tired of them. Consequently, the sale consisted of a lot of "this and that" and not a complete set of anything. Most of the goods had just been dragged out of the storage shed in the backyard of the rental she lived in until she passed away, and set out on various card and picnic tables at yard-sale prices.

In the middle of one long table, I spotted an old metal table lamp with a dented shade that wasn't pleasing to the eye. The price quoted was $3, but I complained about the dent and got it reduced to $2. I lived in Algiers Point, a historical area of New Orleans on the west bank of the Mississippi River, and thought it would fit right in among my parlor plants if I just spray painted it the same aqua color my other accents bore. Though electric, it was certainly old enough to fit in with my other antiques.

When I got to get a look at the underside of the base, I saw the signature: "Tiffany Studios, New York." I was stunned and immediately set down the can of aqua paint and began yelling for my husband to come and see if he saw what I thought I was seeing.

It was, and after he removed the shade and found the same signature, we jotted down the numbers he also found and ran to the Algiers Point Library. With the librarian's help, we learned that Tiffany made all-bronze lamps during a short period of the early 20th century, and this was one of them. After sending off pictures of various parts of the lamp to a well-known auction house, we were given a tentative appraisal of $2,800 in "as-is" condition. We were excited, but decided, at the time, to keep it in the family (unpainted and with the dent gently removed) and added it, by codicil, to our will.

My cousin was a producer on a popular local TV talk show, and she persuaded me to bring it on camera in a segment called "Garage Sale Treasures." The lamp and the show were big hits. However, it seemed to draw a little too much attention from some of the residents of a neighboring unsavory community; when I walked into a nearby convenience store, the cashier identified me out loud as "that lady on TV with that expensive lamp!"

Instantly, I was the center of attention. It's a small community, and we were the "new bees" and everyone knew which vintage house we had bought. So, we decided it wasn't worth the risk to our dogs who dutifully guarded our house. We wrote another codicil taking the Tiffany out of our will and called one of the many legitimately interested people who contacted us after the show.

We accepted an offer of $1,200 and made a profit of $1,198.

I like that kind of margin.

> — **Lynne Adams Barze**
> **Picayune, Miss.**

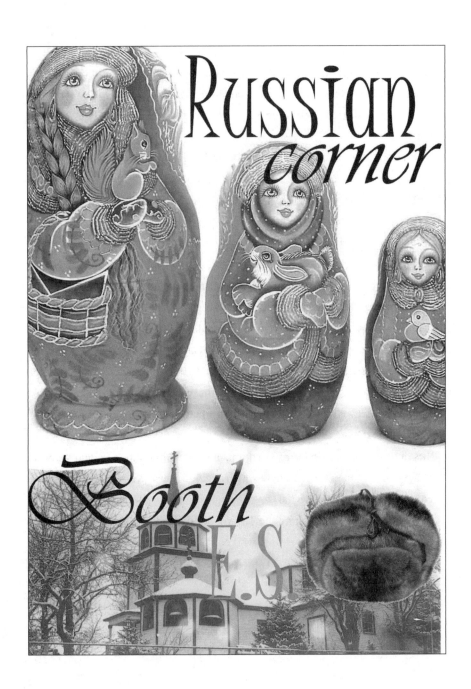

Russian *corner*

Booth

GRANDMOTHER'S RUSSIAN HOME HOLDS FOND MEMORIES

• • • • • • • • •

When I was a little girl, I usually spent summertime in my grandmother's house. It was probably the most remarkable part of my whole year. She lived just outside of a small Russian town called Kursavka. Most of the houses in my grandmother's neighborhood were custom built and handmade with the big clay bricks that were commonly used after World War II. Every house was surrounded by a private fence and had its own individual garden.

Everything in these gardens had been planted and cultivated by the homeowner's hands and primitive garden tools. I remember I used to sneak out of house during late afternoons while my grandmother was taking her naps and play for hours inside a her little barn full of garden tools. What an adventure that was!

Her house contained two rooms connected to the big "cold" room by a little hallway. The first room was a combination of a kitchen, dining room and bedroom. Most of the space in this room was taken up by the stove, which was made out of bricks and an iron top with a big hole in the middle. The hole was covered by three different sizes of iron covers that stacked on top of each other, as if they were nesting dolls.

Early in the morning, my little body was lost somewhere between the soft and comfortable handmade pillows and mattress called a "Perina," filled with chicken feathers carefully trimmed of their sharp ends. It was a large mattress, but very light and soft, the pillows as well were made of the same feathers. At this time of day, my mother would start the fire, and the magic of the atmosphere would slowly unravel itself. Waking up from this blissful bit of comfort, the stove adjusted for the fit of the pan and water put on to boil, was a daily morning routine that I remember well to this day.

The second room was a combination of a master bedroom/hobby room. The contents of this room were mostly a big bed covered by a beautiful quilt and a colorful tapestry of a deer with big, brown eyes, which stared at me from its place on the wall. The centerpiece of every house at this time was an old Russian icon with an oil lamp in front of it. On the wall nearby hung the seven-day cuckoo clock. This happened to be the biggest entertainment in the house for me. Every hour, no matter where I was in the house, I would watch the little bird trying unsuccessfully to escape the confinement of the clock.

But the most amazing and biggest mystery in the house was the "cold" room. To this day, I have no idea how, even in the hottest days of summer, this room would always stay cold (and what kind of pottery my grandmother used to keep the milk in, which kept it cold and fresh for days on end).

The walls in both rooms were filled with old family photos, one of which was my great-grandfather with his big, curly mustache, smiling and waving at me. Once upon a time, he was owner of a big manufacturing company in the pre-revolutionary Russia. Another photo was of my grandfather wearing his vintage

military uniform. He was a hero who lost his life in action during World War II. Also along these walls were plenty of photos of family members I never knew or could remember.

Behind the garden and further beyond the fence was a big piece of land belonging to my grandmother. Sunflowers, corn and many fruit trees were scattered and growing there. If you kept walking, you would stumble across a naturally made canyon near the corner of the property. What you would see on the opposite wall of the canyon would stop your breath and make you feel as if you were a character from a Russian tale. Bits and pieces of minerals that would get washed up by the lake riddled the canyon walls with their bedazzling shapes and sizes, sparkling in the sun as the rays shifted throughout the minerals, flashing brilliant kaleidoscopic colors.

Time passes, and after many of life's tribulations and trials, I finally found a new home and prosperity in America. These fond childhood memories slowly drift back and put a whole new perspective on the things I owned and their true intrinsic value. I'm not sure if there were any genuine antiques in my grandmother's house, but one thing I knew for sure. Without a doubt I grew up surrounded by treasure that any antiques dealer would die for. With this knowledge of what is truly valued and many of thousands of miles away, in the middle of Florida, the "Russian corner" was born.

— **Evguenia Storch**
Orange Park, Fla.

FURNITURE STYLES

Furniture styles can be determined by careful study and remembering what design elements each one embraces. To help you understand what defines each period, here are some of the major design elements for each period.

For more information, prices and identification, read *Antique Trader Antiques & Collectibles 2012 Price Guide*, 28th edition, by Eric Bradley, available at Shop. Collect.com or 800-258-0929.

• • • • • • • •

WILLIAM AND MARY, 1690-1730

The style is named for the English King William of Orange and his consort, Mary. New colonists in America brought their English furniture traditions with them and tried to translate these styles using native woods. Their furniture was practical and sturdy. Lines of this furniture style tend to be crisp, while facades might be decorated with bold grains of walnut or maple veneers, framed by inlaid bands. Moldings and turnings are exaggerated in size.

Turnings are baluster-shaped, and the use of C-scrolls was quite common. Feet found in this period generally are round or oval. One exception to this is known as the Spanish foot, which flares to a scroll. Woods tend to be maple, walnut, white pine or southern yellow pine.

One type of decoration that begins in the William and Mary period and extends through to Queen Anne and Chippendale styles is known as "japanning," referring to a lacquering process that combines ashes and varnish.

Cabinet on stand, continental, walnut, top section with molded cornice with sides extended, panel below, carved cartouche and scrolling stems with flowers; intricately carved paneled door below flanked by two tapered round columns, door with border of bas relief leafage, twin vertical panels with conforming cartouche and leafage; lower section with molded mid-band, single drawer with conforming leaf scroll and flowers, two free-standing front columns with drapery swags, stretcher shelf; twin vertical panels with neo-classic portrait heads, leafage with rosettes; urns with birds below, bun feet, late 19th century; tin plate reinforces top of right front corner; left column with repaired split at top; damage to left top corner of cornice, 68 5/8" h, 31" w, 18" deep, $1,035. *Photo courtesy Sanford Alderfer Auction & Appraisal, Hatfield, Pa.; www.AlderferAuction.com*

QUEEN ANNE, 1720-1760

Evolution of this design style is from Queen Anne's court, 1702 to 1714, and it lasted until the Revolution. This style of furniture is much more delicate than its predecessor. It was one way for the young Colonists to show their own unique style, with each regional area initiating special design elements.

Forms tend to be attenuated in New England. Chair rails were more often mortised through the back legs when made in Philadelphia. New England furniture makers preferred pad feet, while the makers in Philadelphia used triffid feet. Makers in Connecticut and New York often preferred slipper and claw and ball feet.

The most popular woods were walnut, poplar, cherry and maple. Japanned decoration tends to be in red, green and gilt, often on a blue-green field. A new furniture form of this period was the tilting tea table.

CHIPPENDALE, 1755-1790

This period is named for the famous English cabinetmaker, Thomas Chippendale, who wrote a book of furniture designs, "The Gentlemen and Cabinet-Maker's Director," published in 1754, 1755 and 1762. This book gave cabinetmakers real direction, and they soon eagerly copied the styles presented.

Chippendale was influenced by ancient cultures, such as Roman and Gothic influences. Look for Gothic arches, Chinese fretwork, columns, capitals, C-scrolls, S-scrolls, ribbons, flowers, leaves, scallop shells, gadrooning and acanthus leaves.

The most popular wood used in this period was mahogany, with walnut, maple and cherry also present. Legs became straight, and regional differences still existed in design elements, such as feet. Claw and ball feet become even larger and more decorative. Pennsylvania cabinetmakers used Marlborough feet, while other regions favored ogee bracket feet. One of the most popular forms of this period was a card table that sported five legs instead of the four of Queen Anne designs.

FEDERAL (HEPPLEWHITE), 1790-1815

This period reflects the growing patriotism felt in the young American states. The desire to develop their

Chair, Egyptian Revival, with carved winged figure, pierced skirt and light rose upholstery, 19th/20th century, 39" x 24" x 21", $1,680.
Photo courtesy Rago Arts and Auction Center, Lambertville, N.J.;
www.RagoArts.com

own distinctive furniture style was apparent.

Stylistically, it also reflects the architectural style known as Federal, where balance and symmetry were extremely important. Woods used during this period were mahogany and mahogany veneer, but other native woods, such as maple, birch or satin-wood, were used. Reflecting the architectural ornamentation of the period, inlays were popular, as were carving and even painted highlights.

The motifs used for inlay included bellflowers, urns, festoons, acanthus leaves and pilasters, to name but a few. Inlaid bands and lines were also popular and often used in combination

Highboy, William and Mary, maple and ebonized in two sections; upper section with two small drawers over three wide graduated drawers, brass drop handles; lower section with frieze drawer flanked by two deep drawers, trumpet-turned legs joined by flat shaped stretcher, short turned feet, 60" h, 37 3/4" w, 17 1/2" deep, $3,450. *Photo courtesy Sanford Alderfer Auction & Appraisal, Hatfield, Pa.; www.AlderferAuction.com*

with other inlay. Legs of this period tend to be straight or tapered to the foot. The foot might be a simple extension of the leg, or bulbous or spade shaped.

Two new furniture forms were created in this period: the sideboard and the worktable. Expect to find a little more comfort in chairs and sofas, but not very thick cushions or seats.

When a piece of furniture is made in England, or styled after an English example, it may be known as Hepplewhite. The time frame is the same. Robert Adam is credited with creating

Corner cupboard, New England Sheraton, birch and maple, upper case with molded cornice and canted sides centering a pair of glass paneled doors opening to two fixed shelves, fitted to the lower case having a pair of cupboard doors opening to a shelf. Base with shaped and arched apron, 79" h, 46 1/2" w, 23 1/2" deep. Early refinished medium-brown surface. Retains original backboards with hand-cut nails, original feet, $2,300. *Photo courtesy James D. Julia Auctioneers, Fairfield, Maine; www.JuliaAuctions.com*

was by Alice Hepplewhite, and titled "The Cabinet Maker and Upholsterer's Guide," published in 1788, 1789 and 1794.

SHERATON, 1790-1810

The style known as Sheraton closely resembles Federal. The lines are somewhat straighter, and the designs plainer than Federal. Sheraton pieces are more closely associated with rural cabinetmakers.

Woods would include mahogany, mahogany veneer, maple and pine, as well as other native woods. This period was heavily influenced by the work of Thomas Sheraton and his series of books, "The Cabinet Maker and Upholsterer's Drawing Book," from 1791-1794, and "The Cabinet Directory," 1803, "The Cabinet-Maker, Upholsterer," and "General Artist's Encyclopedia" of 1804.

EMPIRE (CLASSICAL), 1805-1830

By the beginning of the 19th century, a new design style was emerging. Known as Empire, it had an emphasis on the classical world of Greece, Egypt and ancient European influences. The American craftsmen began to incorpo-

the style known as Hepplewhite during the 1760s and leading the form. Another English book heavily influenced the designers of the day. This one

rate more flowing patriotic motifs, such as eagles with spread wings.

The basic wood used in the Empire period was mahogany. However, during this period, dark woods were so favored that often mahogany was painted black. Inlays were popular when made of ebony or maple veneer. The dark woods offset gilt highlights, as were the brass ormolu mountings often found in this period. The legs of this period are substantial and more flowing than those found in the Federal or Sheraton periods.

Feet can be highly ornamental, as when they are carved to look like lion's paws, or plain, when they extend to the floor with a swept leg. Regional differences in this style are very apparent, with New York City being the center of the design style, as it was also the center of fashion at the time.

New furniture forms of this period include the sleigh bed, with both headboard and footboard forming graceful arches. Several new forms of tables also came into being, especially the sofa table.

Because the architectural style of the Empire period used big, open rooms, the sofa was now allowed to be in the center of the room, with a table behind it. Former architectural periods found

Bookcase, Victorian, oak with carved vine detail, three leaded-glass doors over three drawers and turned columns, 19th century, 65 3/4″ x 68 1/2″ x 16 1/4″, $2,160. *Photo courtesy Rago Arts and Auction Center, Lambertville, N.J.; www.RagoArts.com*

most furniture placed against the outside perimeter of the walls and brought forward to be used.

VICTORIAN, 1830-1890

The Victorian period as it relates to furniture styles can be divided into several distinct styles. However, not every piece of furniture can be dated or definitely identified, so the generic term "Victorian" will apply to those pieces. Queen Victoria's reign affected the design styles of furniture, clothing and all sorts of items used in daily liv-

Feet

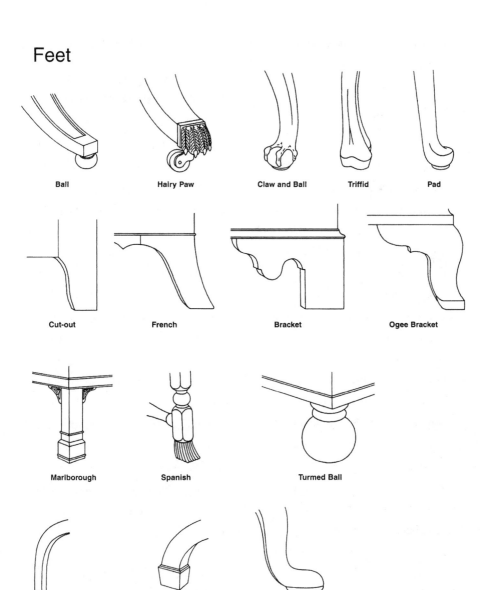

Ball

Hairy Paw

Claw and Ball

Triffid

Pad

Cut-out

French

Bracket

Ogee Bracket

Marlborough

Spanish

Turmed Ball

Spider

Spade

Snake

ing. Her love of ornate styles is well known. When thinking of the general term, think of a cluttered environment, full of heavy furniture, plants, heavy fabrics, china and glassware.

FRENCH RESTORATION, 1830-1850

This is the first sub-category of the Victoria era. This style is best simplified as the plainest of the Victorian styles. Lines tend to be sweeping, undulating curves. It is named for the style that was popular in France as the Bourbons tried to restore their claim to the French throne, from 1814 to 1848. The Empire (Classical) period influence is felt, but French Restoration lacks some of the ornamentation and fussiness of that period. Design motifs continue to reflect an interest in the classics of Greece and Egypt. Chair backs are styled with curved and concave crest rails, making them a little more comfortable than earlier straight-back chairs.

The use of bolster pillows and more upholstery is starting to emerge. The style was only popular in clusters, but it did entice makers from larger metropolitan areas, such as Boston and New Orleans, to embrace the style.

THE GOTHIC REVIVAL PERIOD, 1840-1860

This is relatively easy for collectors to identify. It's one of the few styles that celebrates elements found in the corresponding architectural themes: turrets, pointed arches and quatrefoils — designs found in 12th through 16th centuries that were adapted to this furniture style. The furniture shelving form known as an étagère was born in this period, allowing Victorians to have more room to display their treasured collections. Furniture that had mechanical parts was also embraced in this era.

Makers of this period preferred walnut and oak woods, with some use of mahogany and rosewood. The scale ranged from large and grand to small and petite, while carved details gave dimension and interest.

ROCOCO REVIVAL, 1845-1870

This design style features the use of scrolls, either in a "C" shape or the more fluid "S" shape. Carved decoration in the form of scallop shells, leaves and flowers, particularly roses and acanthus, further add to the ornamentation of this style of furniture. Legs and feet are cabriole or scrolling.

Other than what might be needed structurally, it is often difficult to find a straight element in Rococo Revival furniture. The use of marble for tabletops was quite popular, but expect to find the corners shaped to conform to the overall scrolling form. To accomplish all this carving, walnut, rosewood and mahogany were common choices. When lesser woods were used, they were often painted to resemble more expensive woods. Some cast-iron elements can be found on furniture from this period, especially as scrolls. The style began in France and England, but it eventually came to America, where it evolved into two other furniture styles, Naturalistic and Renaissance Revival.

ELIZABETHAN, 1850-1915

This sub-category of the Victorian era is probably the most feminine-influenced style. It also makes use of the new machine-turned spools and spiral profiles that were fast becoming popular with furniture makers. New technology advancements allowed more machined parts to be generated. The addition of flowers, either carved or painted, gave the furniture pieces of this era a softness. Chair backs tend to be high and narrow and have a slight back tilt. Legs vary from straight to baluster- or spindle-turned forms. This period of furniture design saw more usage of needlework upholstery and decoratively painted surfaces.

LOUIS XVI, 1850-1914

One period of the Victorian era that flies away with straight lines is Louis XVI. However, this furniture style is not austere; it is adorned with ovals, arches, applied medallions, wreaths, garlands, urns and other Victorian flourishes. As the period aged, more ornamentation became present on the finished furniture styles. Furniture of this time was made from more expensive woods, such as ebony or rosewood. Walnut was popular around the 1890s. Other dark woods were featured, often to contrast lighter ornaments. Expect to find straight or fluted and slightly tapered legs.

NATURALISTIC, 1850-1914

This furniture period takes the scrolling effects of the Rococo Revival designs and adds more flowers and fruits to the styles. More detail is given to the leaves — so much that one can tell if they are to represent grape, rose or oak leaves.

Technology advances enhanced this design style, as manufacturers developed a way to laminate woods together. This layered effect was achieved by gluing thin layers together, with the grains running at right angles on each new layer. The thick panels created were then steamed in molds to create the illusion of carving. The woods used as a basis for the heavy ornamentation were mahogany, walnut and some rosewood. Upholstery of this period is often tufted, eliminating any large, flat surface. The name of John Henry Belter is often connected with this period, for it was when he did some of his best design work. John and Joseph W. Meeks also enjoyed success with laminated furniture. Original labels bearing these names are sometimes found on furniture pieces from this period, giving further provenance.

RENAISSANCE REVIVAL, 1850-1880

Furniture made in this style period reflects how cabinetmakers interpreted 16th- and 17th-century designs. Their motifs range from curvilinear and florid early in the period to angular and almost severe by the end of the period. Dark woods, such as mahogany and walnut, were primary, with some use of rosewood and ebony. Walnut veneer panels were a real favorite in the 1870s designs. Upholstery, usually of a more generous nature, was often incorporated into this design style. Ornamentation and high-relief carving included flowers, fruits, game, classical busts, acanthus scrolls, strapwork, tassels and masks. Architectural motifs, such as pilasters, columns, pediments, balusters and brackets, are another prominent design feature. Legs are usually cabriole or have substantial turned profiles.

NÉO-GREEK, 1855-1885

This design style easily merges with both the Louis XVI and Renaissance Revival. It is characterized by elements reminiscent of Greek architecture, such as pilasters, flutes, column, acanthus, foliate scrolls, Greek

Legs

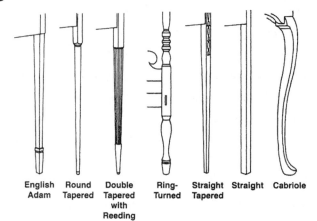

English
Adam

Round
Tapered

Double
Tapered
with
Reeding

Ring-
Turned

Straight
Tapered

Straight

Cabriole

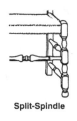

Split-Spindle

Ring-turned

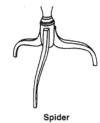

Spider

Snake

Hardware

Bail Handle

Teardrop Pull

Oval Brass

Brass

Pressed Glass

Wooden Knob

Eagle Brass

key motifs and anthemion high-relief carving. This style originated with the French but was embraced by American furniture manufacturers. Woods are dark and often ebonized. Ornamentation may be gilded or bronzed. Legs tend to be curved to scrolled or cloven-hoof feet.

EASTLAKE, 1870-1890

This design style is named for Charles Locke Eastlake, who wrote a popular book in 1872 called "Hints on Household Taste." It was originally published in London. One of his principles was the relationship between function, form and craftsmanship. Shapes of furniture from this style tend to be more rectangular. Ornamentation was created through the use of brackets, grooves, chamfers and geometric designs. American furniture manufacturers were enthusiastic about this style, since it was so easy to adapt for mass production. Woods used were again dark, but more native woods, such as oak, maple and pine, were incorporated. Legs and chair backs are straighter, often with incised decoration.

ART FURNITURE, 1880-1914

This period represents furniture designs gone mad, almost an "anything goes" school of thought. The style embraces both straight and angular with some pieces that are much more fluid, reflecting several earlier design periods. This era saw the wide usage of turned moldings and dark woods, but this time stained to imitate ebony and lacquer. The growing Oriental influence is seen in furniture from this period, including the use of bamboo, which was imported and included in the designs. Legs tend to be straight; feet tend to be small.

ARTS & CRAFTS, 1895-1915

The Arts & Crafts period of furniture represents one of the strongest trends for current collectors. Quality period Arts & Crafts furniture is available through most of the major auction houses. And, for those desiring the look, good quality modern furniture is also made in this style.

The Arts & Crafts period furniture is generally rectilinear, and a definite

Construction Details

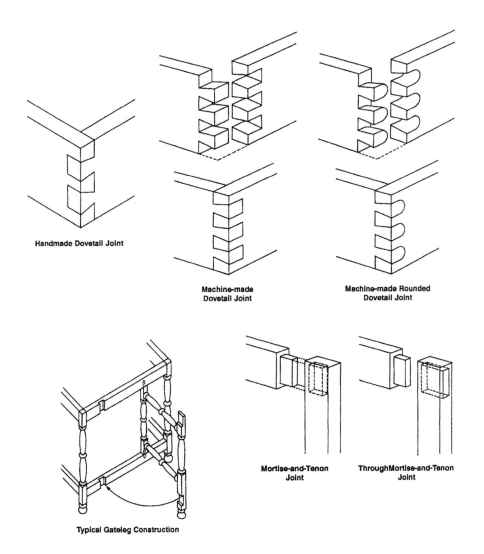

Handmade Dovetail Joint

Machine-made
Dovetail Joint

Machine-made Rounded
Dovetail Joint

Typical Gateleg Construction

Mortise-and-Tenon
Joint

ThroughMortise-and-Tenon
Joint

correlation is seen between form and function.

The primary influences of this period were the Stickley brothers (especially Gustav, Leopold and John George), Elbert Hubbard, Frank Lloyd Wright and Harvey Ellis. Their furniture designs often overlapped into architectural and interior design, including rugs, textiles and other accessories.

Wood used for Arts & Crafts furniture is primarily oak. Finishes were natural, fumed or painted. Hardware was often made in copper. Legs are straight and feet are small, if present at all, as they were often a simple extension of the leg. Some inlay of natural materials was used, such as silver, copper and abalone shells.

Cabinet, Arts & Crafts style, single door with strap hinges and original hardware, interior contains one shelf, refinished, 20" w x 20" d x 29" h, very good condition, $450.
Photo courtesy of Treadway Toomey Galleries, Cincinnati and Oak Park, Ill.; www.treadwaygallery.com

ART NOUVEAU, 1896-1914

Just as the Art Nouveau period is known for women with long hair, flowers and curves, so is Art Nouveau furniture. The Paris Exposition of 1900 introduced furniture styles reflecting what was happening in the rest of the design world, such as jewelry and silver. This style of furniture was not warmly embraced, as the sweeping lines were not conducive to mass production.

The few manufacturers that did interpret it for their factories found interest to be slight in America. The French held it in higher esteem. Legs tend to be sweeping or cabriole. Upholstery becomes slimmer.

ART DECO, 1920-1945

The Paris "L'Exposition Interna-

finest example of Art Deco architecture, and those same straight lines and gentle curves are found in furniture.

Makers used expensive materials, such as veneers, lacquered woods, glass and steel. The cocktail table first enters the furniture scene during this period. Upholstery can be vinyl or smooth fabrics. Legs are straight or slightly tapered; chair backs tend to be either low or extremely high.

MODERNISM, 1940-PRESENT

Furniture designed and produced during this period is distinctive, as it represents the use of some new materials, like plastic, aluminum and molded laminates.

The Bauhaus and the Museum of Modern Art heavily influenced some designers. In 1940, the museum organized competitions for domestic furnishings. Designers Eero Saarien and Charles Eames won first prize for their designs. A new chair design combined the back, seat and arms together as one unit. Tables were designed that incorporated the top, pedestal and base as one. Shelf units were also designed in this manner.

Magazine stand (no. 80), Roycroft, tall trapezoidal, carved Orb and Cross mark, 64" x 17 3/4" sq., $18,000. *Photo courtesy Rago Arts and Auction Center, Lambertville, N.J.; www.RagoArts.com*

tional des Arts Décorative et Industriels Modernes" became the mantra for designs of everything in this period. Lines are crisp, with some use of controlled curves. The Chrysler Building in New York City remains among the

CHAPTER 5

JEWELRY

This Fantastic Find turned out to be an early 20th-century Collet necklace composed of 25 graduated cushion-outline cabochon Ceylon sapphires with an estimated weight of 64 carats plus 5 carats of 50 round diamonds, all Old European cut. The gems are set in 25, 18-karat yellow gold bezels and 50 platinum bezels worth an appraised $38,500.

HOT AUCTION HALL BEGAT A HOT FIND

• • • • • • • • •

I started attending the Brown Brothers Auction House, located in Buckingham, Pa., about 26 years ago. During the summer months, the auction switches from Saturdays to Thursdays.

There is nothing quite like the dog days of summer with temperatures in the 90s and you are in a former dance hall dating back to the 1900s with nothing more than ceiling fans and open windows. However, this is where one specific Thursday season in 1986 I made the find of my antiquing lifetime.

I'll never forget looking at all the table items, furniture and box lots, as I did every Thursday during the one-hour preview time, before I eventually went to the tray lots of just about anything and everything you could imagine.

On one specific tray lot was a necklace of small white diamonds with other stones of a unique blue color. When I asked to see it, upon further investigation the blue colored stones appeared to be glass. Since I was always looking for something for my wife, I thought if I could purchase this at the "right" price, I would then have someone take it apart, throw away the glass stones, and use the little white (I hoped the piece was unmarked) stones to have a tennis bracelet made for my wife.

The auction started at 4 p.m. but the tray lots did not come up for sale until 6:30 p.m. Finally as was allowed, I picked the necklace from the tray and the bidding began. Believe it or not, the bidding opened at $1! Several people were bidding with me and it began to slow down and then stopped with my last bid of $200. Thinking I had purchased it, another bidder at the very last moment offered a $210 bid. What should I do, really wanting it for my wife? I became caught up in the auction emotion (which all auctioneers love to see) and finally won the piece, but had to pay the $700 final bid!

Now auction remorse started to set in. I probably could have bought a nice tennis bracelet for a lot less than $700 at a retail store. But I wanted it and left that night pretty excited, not knowing what was yet to be discovered.

The next morning I took the bracelet to my local jewelry store to get an idea on the design of the tennis bracelet. When the jeweler took one look at the necklace he became visibly excited. I was not sure what was going on. But when he was able to catch his breath, he told me what the blue "glass" stones really were: rare cornflower blue Ceylon cabochon sapphires!

I am enclosing a picture of the necklace along with a GIA appraisal complete with description. And by the way, my wife loves the necklace and still has never gotten the tennis bracelet.

— **Christopher Mahle Sr.**
Washington Crossing, Pa.

EPILOGUE: An appraisal report accompanying this Favorite Find shows the would-be tennis bracelet is an early 20th century Collet necklace composed of 25 graduated cushion-outline cabochon Ceylon sapphires with an estimated weight of 64 carats, plus 5 carats of 50 round diamonds, all Old European cut. The gems are set in 25 18-karat yellow gold bezels and 50 platinum bezels worth an appraised $38,500.

TARNISH BELIES TREASURE AMID JUNK
•••••••••

My most recent favorite find was a 50-cent jewelry box with assorted kids' necklaces and a vintage Navajo silver and turquoise bookmark. It was all black with tarnish and didn't look like much, but I could see it was signed on the back. We were able to make a very good profit on it by selling it for $137, after the commission from the gallery. Amazing what you find mixed in with junk. It was a very pleasant day of shopping for me.

— **Dayna McDaniel**
via e-mail

JEWELRY BOX GEMS
•••••••••

I was sitting at home one night, visiting with our grown son, when the phone rang at about 9. A lady asked if I bought antiques, and I said that I did. She said she was leaving town and had some items for sale. I told her I would be by first thing in the morning. This was unacceptable, as she was leaving town early in the morning; I would have to come tonight.

My son and I drove over about 10 p.m. I never saw so much junk furniture.

She took us into the back bedroom, and I spotted a jewelry box on the dresser and asked if it was for sale. She said that it was but thought it might be too expensive, and I probably would not want it. I asked the price and she quoted $65. I made a note of it on my notepad. It was marked Wave Crest and was about 4 inches in diameter with hand-painted lid, all in mint condition.

We then went into the front bedroom, and there was a 6-inch jewelry box with a beautiful hand-painted Victorian girl on the lid. I asked if it was for sale, and she said it was, but it was not as valuable as the smaller one, and it was $35. It was signed CFM and also was in mint condition. I made a note of it, too.

I could not find any other items in the house worth hauling off. I offered her $300 for everything in the house. She wanted cash as she was leaving town before the banks opened in the morning. I happened to have that amount in my pocket. We loaded up everything, including the two boxes and went home. We still have the two boxes in our private collection.

— **Jim & Becky Mecklin**
via e-mail

TIME TO HUNT FOR MORE BREITLINGS

· · · · · · · · ·

At an estate auction, I bought a 1941 Breitling Premier Chronograph wrist watch. I had no idea what it was. My winning bid was $15 with a 10 percent buyer's premium.

I listed it on eBay with a starting bid of $1.99. To my shock and amazement, within 24 hours it was up to $500, and the final bid was $919. I've been selling on eBay for 10 years under the name of Chuckhole, and that's my best deal ever.

— **Dave Allen**
Forks, Wash.

FINDER GUESSES BEADED ITEM
MAY BE A HAIR COMB

• • • • • • • • •

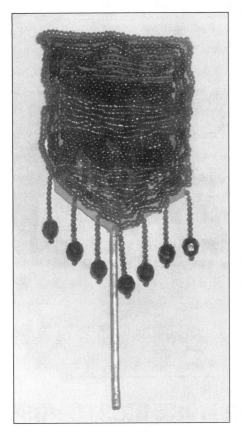

I am in an assisted living facility. To help out, I volunteered to clean the leaves on the large plants in all the public rooms. After two weeks of work, I was cleaning one of the last trees. One had a lot of dead leaves and trash around the base of the trunk.

In cleaning out the leaves and trash, my hand hit something hard under the dirt. I pulled out the item, then cleaned and reattached the loose beads. There are approximately 34 rows of tiny black and coral beads. They look as if they are attached to the backing by hand.

Seven jets (gems) are hanging from the backing by small, beaded strings. The stick was faded gold, so I repainted it. I then encased the item in a deep frame. The stick is 6 inches and runs full length to support the entire item. The beaded body is 3 inches high and 2 1/2 inches wide.

What is it? My guess is that it is a handmade hair comb that was used to secure a bun of hair on the back or top of the head. My guess seems plausible, but other folks have given suggestions, such as a family piece used for identification.

How long it remained under the dirt is unknown. I would like to hear from others who can accurately identify this item.

Thank you for all the hard work you have put into the *Antique Trader*. I have subscribed to the paper forever. I think it is great in its present form. I love it!

— Mary M. Wetzel Tomalka
North Carolina

SURPRISE!
A TIFFANY DREAM COMES TRUE

•••••••••

My favorite find was in a little shop in Hermosa Beach, Calif., about 30-plus years ago. Being a self-described patriot, I found a little money clip that had the American flag and an eagle on it. I kept it in a box with other items that I loved. Back in 1998 or 1999, there was a national emergency and the public was being asked for help.

At that time our nation was in a recession, and even worse in southern California. I went through my clothing and my dresser drawers to find all I could to send.

As I was going through a drawer I pulled out that little box, and out fell that money clip. I'd never really given it a close look, except for the eagle and flag, so I turned it over. I walked over to the window to get extra light, put on my glasses and turned the money clip over to look at the back. To my great surprise, the back was engraved with the words: "Tiffany Studios St. Louis World Fair 1904 Patent Pending."

At this point, I must say that my husband and I owned a retail lighting store and sold a lot of Tiffany lamp reproductions, but we'd never had the good fortune of finding a true Tiffany lamp to buy (and couldn't have afforded it in any event).

So now we have a Tiffany and feel privileged. I have no idea as to its value and would love to know. No matter how much it's worth, it is our family joy to own it.

— Paula Ross Anding
via e-mail

'SPARKLY' YIELDS A BIG FIND

· · · · · · · ·

"Shiny" and "sparkly" have always diverted me from my intended mission, whatever that may be. In this case, I was checking out at a church garage sale last year when something sparkly caught my eye. It was a gold watch with 32 shiny stones on its face. The name on it was Raymond Weil, which I recognized as a good brand.

I figured $6 wouldn't be a bad investment if it turned out to be real, and not too much to swallow if not. My jeweler couldn't tell me anything about it, but he did put in a new battery for $8. However, the pin on the side wouldn't move, so the time couldn't be changed. Pretty watch, but maybe not a good one.

New year. New jeweler. The battery was turned right side up and the watch works great, and it is a real Raymond Weil worth about $600.

That was my monetary great find. But the best, best find was when I was about 7 years old. It was at a garage sale—the first time I'd ever heard of such a thing (this was, ahem, in the '50s). My mom loved pottery, having been schooled in the fabulous Ohio pottery since Day One. I found a tiny green vase at that sale that cost me my entire week's allowance — 25¢ — for her for Mother's Day. Once I was grown, I could appreciate why and how much Mom treasured the perfect, signed and dated little Rookwood vase.

— **Lisa Freter Mull**
Lakewood, Colo.

THE DISCOVERIES JUST KEPT COMING

· · · · · · · · ·

On some Sunday afternoon, we were browsing in our local antiques mall. At that time, my wife was collecting items for our dresser. She found a gold gilded metal jewelry box and bought it for $2.

On the way home, she started removing the cloth lining. When we got home we were $350 richer.

I decided to kill time in an antiques shop near where I was having my car serviced. We live in apple country, and I have a collection of old metal apple peelers. I found what looked like an old wooden peeler, and it was complete. I bought it for $12.

Later, when I was looking through some of my books, I found a picture of the same peeler. It said it was Shaker and used to peel apples, pears, and potatoes. It was listed at $480. It is now part of my apple peeler collection.

— **Willard Chapman**
Yucaipa, Calif.

WORLD OF TREASURE
FOUND IN ONE GARAGE

· · · · · · · · ·

I watch the local paper for garage sales and go to all of them. A few years ago, I saw an ad for a sale that was out in the country quite a ways, and the directions were not good. The ad said the sale was at the old Wilson house, and I knew where that was.

At the time I had a resale shop, and after I closed at 4 p.m. I made my way to the sale. An older lady in her early 50s was sitting in the shade in front of a large double garage. A few items were scattered on the ground in front of the garage. Most of what was for sale was still packed in boxes in the garage.

I asked the lady how the sale was going and she said, "Not worth a darn. I've only had two shoppers all day, and they only spent 50 cents."

She seemed downhearted about the results of her sale. She told me her mother had passed away 10 years ago and she had packed everything in the house and stored it in the garage and rented the house to a family with three small children. They had been excellent renters for 10 years. They'd asked her recently if there was any way they could use the garage, and she told them she would have a sale and clean it out so they could use it.

She said, "I'll gladly take $100 for everything in the garage so I can get this over with."

There were several good tools and a Craftsman vise that had been unpacked, and I told her I would be glad to give her $100 for everything.

She said, "Thank you! Now I can get back to Houston, Texas, where I live." She then made me promise to be sure and clean out the garage completely because she had told her renters she would have it ready for them to use.

After hauling four pickup loads to my resale shop, I finally loaded the last box onto my truck. It was a large box filled with red velvet curtains with tassels, and they were very musty smelling. I decided I would take them to the dump the very next time I went. My wife changed my mind. She said if we could get the musty smell out of them, she would make stuffed animals out of them.

We were hanging them over the clothesline when I noticed a small drawstring bag pinned into the back of one of the curtains with a rusty safety pin. I thought, at first, it was the rings for the tiebacks for the curtains. Then I decided to take a look in the bag.

The first thing I found was an Iranian gold piece, about the size of a silver dollar, with a catalog value of $350. The next item in the bag was a piece of jewelry shaped like a sword, with a diamond in the center. It was 18-karat gold, and the diamond was a quarter carat. The local jeweler gave me $450 for it.

The last item in the bag was what looked like a silver ring, with what looked like diamonds in it. I had the local jeweler appraise it for me. When he told me it was worth $10,000, I nearly fainted.

I asked him why they would set diamonds in silver and he said, "It's not silver, It's platinum!"

When I put the ring in an auction it brought $8,600. Not a bad investment for $100!!

— **John Nickle**
Rusk, Texas

BOX LOT BRACELET
A CHERISHED MEMORY

It was a rainy Saturday, and I had convinced my sister to accompany me to a local auction. At that time I was interested in old jewelry, and the sale bill had listed some very nice pieces, as well as some items in which my sister was interested.

The rain drizzled as we walked around with our umbrellas, looking at the items for sale. What a miserable day for an outdoor sale!

We eventually found the jewelry area where the costume jewelry was in numbered bags, as is the custom in our area. The best jewelry was displayed in a locked glass case, and when they finally got around to selling those pieces, they were sold as "choice," meaning the winning bidder could choose as many pieces as he wanted at the bidding price per item.

The pieces were going for prices far higher than I was able to pay, but I just kept hanging in there, hoping they would get close to my comfort level.

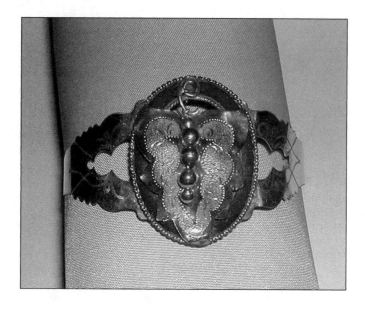

Finally, they were down to the last few pieces when the rain really began coming down. At that point, they decided to sell the remaining pieces as one lot. Because of the weather, the bidders had thinned out quickly, and I was able to buy the remainder for a price that broke down to about 50 cents per item.

Among the pieces I was fortunate to obtain was the beautiful bracelet seen in the attached photo (shown on page 133).

I'm a member of Alliance Chapter of the National Society Daughters of the American Revolution, and a recent meeting featured a local jewelry dealer/appraiser as speaker. We had been invited to bring a piece of jewelry to be appraised if we wished. Of course, I thought of the bracelet. It was appraised at $1,500 to $2,000.

I was thrilled to say the least!

Thank you for the opportunity to tell my little story.

— **Celia G. (Smith) Snyder**
Urbana, Ill.

JEWELRY STYLES

Jewelry has been a part of every culture throughout time. It is often reflective of the times, as well as social and aesthetic movements, with each piece telling its own story through hidden clues that, when interpreted, will help solve the mysteries surrounding them.

Jewelry is generally divided into periods and styles. Additionally, there are recurring style revivals, which are interpretations of an earlier period, such as the Egyptian Revival that took place in the early and late 1800s, and then again in the 1920s. For more jewelry information, prices and identification, read *Warman's Jewelry*, 4th edition, by Kathy Flood, available at Shop.Collect.com or 800-258-0929.

• • • • • • • • •

GEORGIAN, 1760-1837

Fine jewelry from this period is quite desirable, but few good-quality pieces have found their way to auction in recent years. Sadly, much jewelry from this period has been lost.

VICTORIAN, 1837-1901

Queen Victoria of England ascended the throne in 1837 and remained queen until her death in 1901. The Victorian period is a long and prolific one, abundant with many styles of jewelry. It warrants being divided into three sub-periods: Early or Romantic period dating from 1837-1860; Mid or Grand period dating from 1860-1880; and Late or Aesthetic period dating from 1880-1901.

Sentiment and romance were significant factors in Victorian jewelry. Often, jewelry and clothing represented love and affection, with symbolic motifs such as hearts, crosses, hands, flowers, anchors, doves, crowns, knots, stars, thistles, wheat, garlands, horseshoes and moons.

The materials of the time were also

Earrings, yellow gold, turquoise and seed pearls, circa 1880, containing numerous graduated round white seed pearls and graduated turquoise cabochons, in a fitted leather box. 10.20 dwts., $2,928. *Photo courtesy Leslie Hindman Auctioneers, Chicago; www.LeslieHindman.com*

abundant and varied. They included silver, gold, diamonds, onyx, glass, cameo, paste, carnelian, agate, coral, amber, garnet, emeralds, opals, pearls, peridot (a green gemstone), rubies, sapphires, marcasites, cut steel, enameling, tortoise shell, topaz, turquoise, bog oak, ivory, jet, hair, gutta percha and vulcanite.

Sentiments of love were often expressed in miniatures. Sometimes they were representative of deceased loved ones, but often the miniatures were of the living. Occasionally, the miniatures depicted landscapes, cherubs or religious themes.

Hair jewelry was a popular expression of love and sentiment. The hair of a loved one was placed in a special compartment in a brooch or a locket, or used to form a picture under a glass compartment. Later in the mid-19th century, pieces of jewelry were made completely of woven hair. Individual strands of hair would be woven together to create necklaces, watch chains, brooches, earrings and rings.

In 1861, Queen Victoria's husband, Prince Albert, died. The queen went into mourning for the rest of her life, and Victoria required that the royal court wear black. This atmosphere spread to the populace and created a demand for mourning jewelry.

Mourning jewelry is typically black. When it first came into fashion, it was made from jet. By 1850, there were dozens of English workshops making jet brooches, lockets, bracelets and necklaces. As the supply of jet dwindled, other materials were used, such as vulcanite, gutta percha, bog oak and French jet.

By the 1880s, the somber mourning jewelry was losing popularity. Fashions had changed, and the clothing was simpler and had an air of delicacy. The Industrial Revolution, which had begun in the early part of the century, was now in full swing, and machine-manufactured jewelry was affordable to the working class.

EDWARDIAN, 1890-1920

The Edwardian period takes its name England's King Edward VII. Though he ascended the throne in 1901, he and his wife, Alexandria of Denmark, exerted influence over the period before and after his ascension. The 1890s was known as La Belle Epoque. This was a time known for ostentation and extravagance. As the years passed, jewelry became simpler and smaller. Instead of wearing one large brooch, women were often found wearing several small lapel pins.

In the early 1900s, platinum, diamonds and pearls were prevalent in the jewelry of the wealthy, while paste was being used by the masses to imitate the real thing. The styles were reminiscent of the neo-classical and rococo motifs. The jewelry was lacy and ornate, feminine and delicate.

ARTS & CRAFTS, 1890-1920

The Arts & Crafts movement was focused on artisans and craftsmanship. There was a simplification of form where the material was secondary to the design. Guilds of artisans banded together. Some jewelry was mass-produced, but the most highly prized examples of this period are handmade and signed by their makers. The pieces were simple and at times abstract.

They could be hammered, patinated and acid etched. Common materials were brass, bronze, copper, silver, blister pearls, freshwater pearls, turquoise, agate, opals, moonstones, coral, horn, ivory, base metals, amber, cabachon-cut garnets and amethysts.

ART NOUVEAU, 1895-1910

In 1895, Samuel Bing opened a shop called "Maison de l'Art Nouveau" at 22 Rue de Provence in Paris. Art Nouveau designs in the jewelry were character-ized by a sensuality that took on the forms of the female figure, butterflies, dragonflies, peacocks, snakes, wasps, swans, bats, orchids, irises and other exotic flowers. The lines used whiplash curves to create a feeling of lushness and opulence.

1920S-1930S

Costume jewelry began its steady ascent to popularity in the 1920s. Since it was relatively inexpensive to produce, there was mass production.

Pendant-necklace, black opal, diamond and 14-karat gold, Arts and Crafts style, the delicate fancy-link gold chain fitted with an oblong gold slide decorated with tiny pine cones and leaves and enclosing an oblong black opal, suspending an ornate, long gold-frame pendant with open leafy scrolls with tiny pine cones flanking a large almond-shaped black opal above an openwork spear-point frame set with five old European-cut diamonds suspending a black opal teardrop, mark of William Bramley, Montreal, and "14B," 15" l, $17,625.

Bracelet, 1960s, "Asian Princess" figural links with simulated jade spirals, amethyst crystals and faux pearls, unmarked Selini, 7 1/2" x 1 7/8", $175-$300.
Photo courtesy Kathy Flood

The sizes and designs of the jewelry varied. Often, it was worn a few times, disposed of and then replaced with a new piece. It was thought of as expendable, a cheap throwaway to dress up an outfit. Costume jewelry became so popular that it was sold in both upscale stores and "five and dimes."

During the 1920s, fashions were often accompanied by jewelry that drew on the Art Deco movement, which got its beginning in Paris at the "Exposition Internationale des Arts Décoratifs et Industriels Modernes" held in 1925.

The idea behind this movement was that form follows function. The style was characterized by simple, straight, clean lines, stylized motifs and geometric shapes. Favored materials included chrome, rhodium, pot metal, glass, rhinestones, Bakelite and celluloid.

One designer who played an important role was Coco Chanel. Though previously reserved for evening wear, Chanel wore jewelry during the day, making it fashionable for millions of other women to do so, too.

With the 1930s came the Depression and the advent of World War II. Perhaps in response to the gloom, designers began using enameling and brightly colored rhinestones to create whimsical birds, flowers, circus animals, bows, dogs and just about every other figural form imaginable.

Earrings. Art Deco Silver and Enamel, screw back, $61.
Photo courtesy Leslie Hindman Auctioneers, Chicago; www.LeslieHindman.com

RETRO MODERN, 1939-1950

Other jewelry designs of the 1940s were big and bold. Retro Modern had a more substantial feel to it, and designers began using larger stones to enhance the dramatic pieces. The jewelry was stylized and exaggerated. Common motifs included flowing scrolls, bows, ribbons, birds, animals, snakes, flowers and knots.

Sterling silver now became the metal of choice, often dipped in a gold wash known as vermeil.

Designers often incorporated patriotic themes of American flags, the V-sign, Uncle Sam's hat, airplanes, anchors and eagles.

POSTWAR MODERN, 1945-1965

This was a movement that emphasized the artistic approach to jewelry making. It is also referred to as Mid-Century Modern. This approach was occurring at a time when the Beat Generation was prevalent. These avant-garde designers created jewelry that was handcrafted to illustrate the artist's own concepts and ideas. The materials often used were sterling, gold, copper, brass, enamel, cabochons, wood, quartz and amber.

1950S-1960S

The 1950s saw the rise of jewelry made purely of rhinestones: necklaces, bracelets, earrings and pins.

The focus of the early 1960s was on clean lines: pillbox hats and A-line dresses with short jackets were a mainstay for conservative women. Large, bold rhinestone pieces were no longer the must-have accessory. They were replaced with smaller, more delicate gold-tone metal and faux pearls with only a hint of rhinestones.

The other end of the spectrum found psychedelic-colored clothing, Nehru jackets, thigh-high miniskirts and go-go boots. These clothes were accessorized with beads, large metal pendants and occasionally big, bold rhinestones. By the late 1960s, there was a movement back to mother nature and the "hippie" look was born. Ethnic clothing, tie-dye, long skirts, fringe and jeans were the prevalent style, and the rhinestone had, for the most part, been left behind.

MEXICAN SILVER, 1930-1970

Mexican silversmiths first made jewelry for tourists. The jewelry had pre-Hispanic and traditional Mexican motifs, as well as some abstract modern designs. Artisans used silver, a combination of silver with brass or copper, alpaca, amethysts, malachite, obsidian, sodalite, tiger's eye, turquoise, abalone, ebony, rosewood and enameling to create their original designs. While hundreds of artists set up their shops in the town of Taxco, Mexico, in the '30s and '40s creating a silversmith guild, there are only a relatively small number of well-known artisans who gained their reputation for their designs and craftsmanship.

CHAPTER 6

MISCELLANEOUS

STEAMER TRUNK A PASSAGEWAY TO WORLD WAR II

• • • • • • • • •

My greatest discovery is the find of a lifetime — I don't ever expect to top it!

One hot summer Saturday in 1983, my husband and I attended an estate sale in

Annapolis, Md. The household goods for a deceased military couple were being auctioned, and there were tons of goodies. We obtained moving/storage boxes full of custom-made draperies, bedspreads, handmade quilts and exquisite table linen, as well as fabulous glassware and trinkets from around the world — all for reasonable prices.

The treasure was a locked steamer trunk that had been in storage since 1943, and the storage locker contents were included in the sale. We bid $40 for the heavy, locked trunk and took it home to wait for Monday to call a locksmith. Because the trunk was so heavy, I was sure it was full of books and perhaps some officer's uniforms. By noon on Sunday, I could control my excitement no longer, and I persuaded my husband to use the ax to remove the lock!

I still tremble when I think of the contents of this wonderful, old Vuitton steamer trunk. One side was for hanging garments — and there, each wrapped in blue paper, hanging on the hangers, were such amazing things. There were three fabulous ladies' wool suits, several cashmere sweaters, angora socks, silk tap panties with side buttons and appliqué, Chinese silk pajamas, a satin-lined, royal-blue velvet opera coat with Elizabethan collar, and cocktail and daytime dresses in the style of the early 1940s — for a lady no larger than size 6.

The other side had two large drawer compartments that contained evening bags, at least a dozen pairs of kid gloves, several pairs of stylish shoes, three kimonos — one in fantastic condition, one so-so, and the last was just a remnant since it had been eaten by moths.

There was an alcohol iron, boxes of fine costume jewelry, gold shirt studs and military medals that had been awarded to the husband. There were cloisonné salt dishes with spoons and matching pepper shakers, several compacts and hand-tooled leather picture frames. One of the frames included a picture of the owner as a child with a silver serpent bracelet on her arm — the bracelet was also in the drawer!

There was a detachable attaché case at the very bottom of the drawers, and this contained personal letters to/from family — even her dog had his own stationery

— lots of photos of the gorgeous couple; the large checkbook from a prominent bank in Washington, D.C., programs from official events at various embassies and diaries of their assignments prior to the war.

I've had a wonderful time sorting, sharing, selling and savoring these treasures. Most of the things were sold over the years, but I still have such warm feelings for the couple that I feel they became part of my family in an odd sort of way. This is without doubt my all-time greatest discovery!

— **Marie Bailey**
Pasadena, Md.

MICKEY JUMPS FOR JOY
· · · · · · · · ·

While garage shopping many years ago, I came across a Mickey Mouse Jack-in-the-box toy piano. The player turns the handle, and Mickey jumps out of the top of the piano.

"How much?" I asked.

"Fifty cents," I was told.

"Does it work?"

The owner turned the handle and Mickey jumped right out.

I said, "I'll take it!"

He said, "75 cents."

"Why?" I asked.

"It works!" he said.

So I paid, and I still have my Mickey Mouse piano with a story behind it.

— **Martha Boles**
Altamonte Springs, Fla.

COMPOSER'S PICTURE RETURNED TO FAMILY

· · · · · · · ·

I love the hunt for treasures, and about six years ago, I found a lot box with postcards and about six studio pictures, all very old.

One was of a beautiful baby, three of older men in uniforms, and an old lady at a spinning wheel. Under the baby picture was a name written in pencil: Leroy Anderson.

I went on the Internet and put the name in. Yes, it was the real Leroy Anderson, the famous composer. He had not changed a bit from this baby picture. He passed away in 1975 and there is a full website with his history and compositions.

I wrote to the website telling them what I found. I also sent copies of the pictures. After two weeks I received an e-mail from his daughter, Barbara. She asked where I found these. How they got to Florida, no one knows. The best find in this group of pictures was the little old lady. Barbara told me she only had a spinning wheel from her grandmother and no pictures.

I told her I would send them to her in Connecticut and did not want anything in return. These were her family members and belonged to her. She sent me a thank-you note with a gift. The treasure in this is having a picture of her grandmother at the spinning wheel. Sometimes it is not material items but a true memory in a picture.

— **Margaret (Peggy) Coffey**
Valrico, Fla.

SHIP LANTERN LIGHTS UP THIS COLLECTOR

· · · · · · · ·

My favorite find was a ship's lantern I bought for $35 and sold for $70.

— **Tom Schutz**
Princeton, W.Va.

DUMP DIG TURNS UP AMBER INKWELL

· · · · · · · · ·

My favorite find is an antique inkwell. While visiting an uncle in Massachusetts some years ago, Uncle Buser (a devout bottle collector) suggested we go digging in an old nearby dump. Off we went, shovels and rakes in hand. Many small items came up, then I raked up the find of the day: an old amber glass inkwell in perfect condition.

Later that week, while visiting the Sturbridge Museum in Sturbridge, Mass., I saw the very same one on exhibit in a glass showcase. I was thrilled. I still have it today.

However, at my age, 82, should I be selling it?

— **Margaret Dozier**
Point Pleasant, N.J.

TREASURED RECIPE FOUND AGAIN

· · · · · · · · ·

As a teenager growing up in the 1950s, I loved to make cookies every Saturday. One of the favorites was peanut butter, and the best recipe came from the Derby Peter Pan Smooth Peanut Butter 1 lb., 12 oz. tin can that had to be opened with the key twisting around the top. Since I thought this item would be available forever, I never wrote down the recipe. Years passed in which making cookies on Saturday wasn't my priority, so when the day came to look for that recipe, I found this item wasn't to be found. Plastic had replaced the tin can, and Derby had sold out to whomever. I tried many peanut butter cookie recipes, but none seemed to be the same.

I had about given up when one day my husband and I were at a flea market, and I spotted the can holding some guy's nails he was selling. Walking up big as life I asked, "How much for that can?" He replied, "You want the whole can?" My comeback was, "I only want the can, not what's inside it." I'm sure he thought he was dealing with a loose-screw woman, but he said, "10 cents."

As I walked away with my treasure, I whispered to my husband, "If he only knew what I would have paid for that can!" Proof of the pudding came when I gave some of the cookies to my excellent baker daughter-in-law and she exclaimed, "That's the best peanut butter cookie I ever had, and I have to have the recipe."

— Nancy Gebauer
Castile, N.Y.

JUNK JAR FANATIC FINDS CHILDHOOD HERO
· · · · · · · · ·

It was Thursday, and as usual, I looked in *The Chronicle* for estate sale ads. One in particular caught my eye. It was in The Heights, one of the oldest parts of town. It sounded promising.

The next morning, I was on my way to The Heights. I arrived at the address. It was an old two-story row house with weathered red brick. It seemed small from the outside. As I entered, I noticed the home had aged wood floors and a musty smell. It was packed with vintage items from furniture to knickknacks, so much so it was even difficult to move around. I made my way around the first floor and decided to go upstairs.

There were three rooms upstairs, and they were just as packed as downstairs. I made my way around the first room and stumbled over something. I caught myself and looked down to see what nearly caused me to fall. It was an old plastic jar. It was like the kind that held those long stick pretzels. It was about 10 inches tall and 5 inches wide and was jam packed, like the rest of the house.

The jar was filled from top to bottom with all sorts of odds and ends. I could see trinkets, bottle caps, key chains, plastic Indians, matchbooks, pieces of paper and so on. Yep, it was my kind of stuff. I picked up the jar and found a price — $15. I carried the jar with me as I explored the rest of the house but did not see anything else I was interested in.

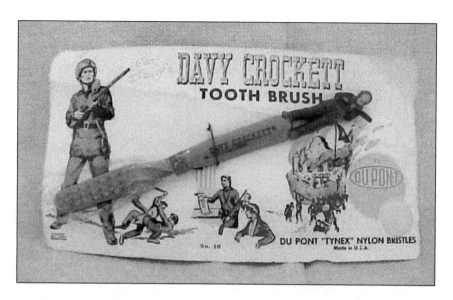

When I took the jar to checkout, the gentleman at the desk said, "So you're the one. I knew someone would take a chance on that jar of junk. He said he could not get the lid off and reminded me all sales were final. I purchased the jar of junk.

When I got home, I managed to get the lid off and attempted to dump out the contents. I turned it over and shook it a few times but nothing came out. So I started taking things out one at a time. I decided to make two piles: one for junk and one for everything else.

About halfway down, I saw a piece of cardboard sticking out. It was gray on one side and faded yellow on the other. I slowly pulled it out. I couldn't believe what I was looking at – a Davy Crockett toothbrush stapled on its original card. It even had cellophane on its brush. It was marked Walt Disney and dated 1956. It took me back to my childhood. I watched all the episodes of Davy Crockett starring Fess Parker. I even had a coonskin cap.

I did some research but couldn't find it mentioned anywhere. So, I decided to sell it on eBay. Even if it sold for $20, I would still make a nice profit. There were 166 salvageable items in the jar of junk at 9 cents apiece.

I started the bidding (for the toothbrush) at $9.99. I had a bid on the first day.

Over the course of a week, the bidding continued at the price steadily climbed. Soon it was $20, and then quickly climbed to $65 where it leveled off. I couldn't believe it. Then, there was that flurry of bidding as time expired. My 9-cent Davy Crockett toothbrush sold for $103.50! Sometimes you just have to take a chance even on a jar of junk.

— **Robert J. Vasko**
Houston, Texas

JUNK-SHOP FIND ENDS
UP AT SOTHEBY'S
• • • • • • • •

About 27 years ago, my late husband and I lived in Manlius, N.Y., a suburb of Syracuse. On quiet Saturday afternoon, we would sometimes visit our favorite junk shop in the village. We never knew what little trinket or treasure we might find.

On one such afternoon, my husband spotted a small wooden box about 4 inches square and deep. He liked the grain of the wood and bought it for $5 and tossed it in the trunk.

When we returned home he opened the little box and found what look liked like a barrel-shaped lens with three glass slides. It looked like some kind of camera.

At the time, my husband was the director of the Center of Instructional Development at Syracuse University, and the photography department reported to him. He took the box to the office and asked the fellows if they could do a little research and see what they could find out about it. A short time later, they came in with an Eastman Kodak book titled *"The First 100 Years of Photography,"* and inside was a picture of our camera called the Tom Thumb. The picture had a dented lens, but ours was in perfect condition.

We called a local camera buff, and he offered us $800 sight unseen. At the time, my mother-in-law lived in Manhattan, and she went to Sotheby's and told them what we'd found. They had a camera auction coming up and said they would be happy to include our camera in the catalog. Through Sotheby's, a gentleman heard of our camera. He had a Tom Thumb but only had one slide. Since the complete camera needed two [slides] and we had three, he offered us $250 for our extra slide. So now the little box that was once thrown in the trunk was carefully wrapped and tenderly carried to New York where it was sold by Sotheby's for more than $2,000, which helped pay for my daughter's wedding.

— **Dolores J. Diamond**
St. Petersburg, Fla.

CHA-CHING: CASH REGISTER IS FIRST IMPULSE BUY
· · · · · · · ·

There have been a few "favorite finds" over my many years of buying, selling and collecting great stuff, but this was the very first.

The year was 1969, and my husband and I, newly married, had moved to our first house in Long Beach, Calif., after a year or so of apartment living. One Saturday, on my way to the grocery store, I passed a yard sale in the neighborhood and decided to stop on the way back to check it out. At this time, yard sales were not something I did as a "religion" as I do now, but this was right on my route back home, so I stopped briefly. I think I bought something little, saw a wide assortment of tools and also fell in love with an old cash register ... but it was priced at $15, and that was a LOT of money in those days for a young couple; after all, our house had only cost $22,000!

I came home and told my husband about the tools, which we needed, as we had a yard and nothing to use in caring for it. A couple of hours later, he went to the sale, bought some of the tools, and when he came back home he asked me if I had noticed the cash register. I said of course I had, absolutely loved it, but didn't feel we could afford it. After talking about it, we decided to go back and get it if it was still available.

Back to the sale we went. By this time it was well after lunch, and the cash register was still there! It proudly became my first "impulse" purchase for my new home, and when I contacted NCR with the serial number found it had been made in 1910. It was a small, ornate register with $1 as the highest amount to ring up, and it was in perfect condition. Even nicer, when I opened the cash drawer I discover a 50-cent coin stuck in the back, so really my extravagant purchase was only $14.50!

— **Sue Shoemaker**
La Habra Heights, Calif.

FAMILY FINDS ITS HERITAGE TWO STATES AWAY

• • • • • • • •

My wife's grandparents had a small Jersey cow dairy farm close to the Canadian border in Washington state in the 1930s and '40s. They bottled their own milk and delivered it around the neighborhood.

They didn't have their name on the milk bottles, but had their name on the bottle caps. We thought it would be nice to have an original cap.

A relative, who still lives on the original place, gave us permission to look in the barn, since my wife's father told us he used to throw those caps around for fun when he was young. We did find some generic caps, but none with their name.

We talked to a local fellow who collected milk bottle caps, and he had one in his collection, but wouldn't sell it.

Well, a couple years went by. We like to attend at least one antique show a year, so we decided to go the Palmer Wirfs show in Portland, Ore. We saw a booth that had several milk bottles and started talking to the dealer, since we were dairy farmers ourselves and have an interest in dairy-related items. My wife told him the story about trying to find her grandfather's bottle cap.

He said he collected caps and asked her the name of the dairy. When she told him, he said he thought he had a few in one of his binders under the table. Sure enough he knew right where to look, and there were seven original bottle caps labeled "Harry VanderMey Phone 396 Sumas Dairy High Grade Jersey Milk" with a picture of a baby on them.

We were thrilled and couldn't believe it. We bought all seven. He said he found them either in Oregon or California. We wonder how they got so far from home. They don't have much monetary value, but they are special to us — something to give to the kids or grandkids.

— **Chuck DeWaard**
Ferndale, Wash.

FAMILY FINDS RELATIVES AT AUCTION
• • • • • • • • •

Besides loving the hunt of antiques, I also delve into my family tree. My favorite find and family tree are very connected!

I am the youngest of 15 children, and my oldest sibling is my brother Leo, 25 years older than me. He was a buyer and seller of antiques and attended many auctions. I loved stopping at his home to see the new purchases. I once stopped to see him and his wife, Doris, taking along our mom.

My brother and his wife lived about 60 miles from me in an area where my ancestors settled when they immigrated from Russia. As my brother, sister-in-law and mom were visiting, I went to the area where they had stuff that they had just purchased. I was snooping through boxes when I came across an oval picture (about 14 inches by 20 inches) of a couple I recognized as my great-grandparents.

I hollered to my brother, "Where did you get the picture of our great-grandparents?!" He called me crazy and said that this wasn't any relative. He said it was just a picture he found behind another picture in an antique oval frame. So we called our mom to come settle our argument, and sure enough, she agreed it was our great-grandparents. I recognized the picture because it was in a book of early settlers I researched at a historical museum.

Anyway, the happy ending was that since I recognized the picture, which he was going to dispose of, he gave me the picture. But he sold me a frame for it

— he was a true dealer! I have since lost my beloved brother, but every time I look at the picture of my great-grandparents, which hangs above a bookcase in my computer room, I treasure the memory of my favorite find, my brother and my great-grandparents.

— Berniece (Bonnie) Rebel
Ness City, Kan.

'I DON'T CARE IF I PAID TOO LITTLE OR TOO MUCH'

• • • • • • • • •

The bigger the antique, the more this collector will love it.

"If it's big or heavy, I know you'll buy it." That's my husband's favorite quote about me when it comes to flea markets, garage sales or antiques fairs.

I can't help myself. I love metal. Solid metal. Not this tin stuff made nowadays. When you have a devotion to solid construction, the weight simply comes with the territory. So, yes, I guess if it's heavy, I buy it.

In Chicago, though, where antiques and unique finds typically come with inflated prices, it's hard for me to find something I can actually afford and justify purchasing. But this summer, I found one of my favorite pieces.

Yes, it's big and heavy and just so coooooool! I saw the beauty across the parking lot. Leaning up against the truck, clean as a bell (no pun intended). It was calling my name — a 50-inch diameter bank sign made of solid metal.

Heavy. Clumsy. Totally my taste! I cautiously, and honestly, walked up to the dealer and said, "I know I won't be able to afford this. But, how much is it?" Expecting pricing around $800, the dealer quoted $450. I said thanks, and thought, well, I could potentially do that. But I waited. I have a tendency to jump at the first offer.

After perusing the rest of the fair, I walked back and said, "How about $350?" To my surprise, he said yes!

I don't care if I paid too little or too much for this. I love this big hunk of a sign. What am I going to do with this? Well, that's a question my husband has given up on asking 10 years ago.

One day this is going to be installed in my yard, surrounded by colorful flowers. Also throughout the yard will be the other metal bells I have collected. They will be attached to posts so visitors can just go "ringing" through my yard. I just hope I don't have neighbors right next door. They might not like that! Here it is! I'm 5-foot, 9-inches tall, so you can see this baby is large. Thankfully!

— **Nancy J. Morris**
Oak Park, Ill.

P.S. I'm a flea market and garage-sale craver! My dream is to win the lotto so that I can simply drive around the United States in search of things to collect — big, heavy things.

NEW BRIDE SHOWS HUBBY
WHY YARD SALES MATTER

• • • • • • • • •

I was a young bride. It was before childbirth, before opening an antiques shop — indeed, before knowing practically anything about antiques. I had married a bona fide pack rat, among whose collections was one of "non-belligerent" souvenirs from World War II.

From the day I met him, I knew he had been looking without success for a "short snorter." To me (and to many people) it sounds like something you drink, rather than something war related.

A short snorter is a wad of money — U.S. dollars, French francs, British pounds or whatever — in which each bill has been autographed by a service person and taped (unfortunately for posterity) to the next. The soldiers signed and exchanged them, and there could be just a few bills or many. The custom, my husband explained to me, apparently began when a famous person visited an army camp and was asked to sign something — anything — and the only paper at hand was a dollar. That may or may not be the real story; nevertheless, he wanted one and had been searching for ages without success. It seemed so unobtainable that he had long stopped looking for it. Neither of us even knew what one would cost.

So here we were at a yard sale — an unpromising yard sale — in Wisconsin. My husband was going his way, and I was going mine. I was hoping to find some unusual heart-shaped antique to add to my collection.

I approached a table filled with tchotchkes and noticed an item that was not only unidentifiable, but also seemed out of place. It was colorful in a sort of muted way and cylindrical — it looked as though you might put cigarettes in it (we were all smokers then) and place it on your coffee table for guests.

"What is that?" I asked the lady while pointing. She shrugged. "I don't know; it was my husband's. He was in the war. I found it with some things after he died," she said.

"Huh, strange isn't it? How much is it?" I asked picking it up while holding my breath, mostly hoping. I was afraid to examine it, which would have meant unrolling the outside. I thought about finding my husband, Richard, but that might make the owner think it was really valuable. Plus, as a newlywed, it would be such fun to surprise him.

"Oh, I don't know. Give me two dollars," the owner said. Remember, this was 1964. Even if it wasn't what I hoped it was, for $2, I could take a chance. I paid the lady, and with it clutched in my hot little hand, I went looking for my guy. Of course, you know the end of the story; you knew it from the first paragraph! All you need to know now is that:

No. 1, it's the antique find I throw out to Richard whenever I need an excuse to "keep looking" while we're out. "Maybe we'll find another short snorter!" and, No. 2, it turned out to be 8 feet long when unravelled! That's somewhat unusual, I'm told, not to mention very hard to frame! But he did it. And it seems it may be worth hundreds of dollars. He's never even seen another one for sale.

So I was a happy bride, and Richard was ecstatic! Don't you just love a story with a happy ending?

— **Bindy Bitterman**
Eureka Antiques,
Evanston, Ill.

SMALL MARBLE ROLLS TOWARD BIG YIELD

• • • • • • • •

My favorite: Vound a marble that was very old and bought it for 5 cents, sold it for $85.

— **Brulo**
via Antique Trader forums

PRINT OWNERS AWAIT AN APPRAISAL

• • • • • • • •

We lived in Algonac, Mich., and went to a church sale. My husband liked a chromolithograph print or "chromo litho" (of course we didn't know that was at the time) by Louis Atkins, of the Grand Canyon and El Tovar. Last winter we were watching "Antiques Roadshow" and saw the same litho appraised for $4,000. We have not been able to get that same appraisal in Michigan. We are still hopeful.

— **Louise Keggs**
via e-mail

FERRIS WHEEL PAPERWEIGHT: $2 GARAGE-SALE SOUVENIR SELLS FOR $200

· · · · · · · · ·

As I am an antiques collector, I will relate to you one of my earlier collec-  tions. While I was an insurance salesman, I traveled from town to town, covering a large area. I stopped at a garage sale and found a paperweight that I purchased for the lowly cost of $2. I didn't pay much attention to it until later, when I went home. While looking it over, I saw a large Ferris wheel on the front of the weight. On the back of the weight, it read that this weight was displayed at the World's Fair in Chicago in the 1800s (exact date unknown). The weight represented the largest Ferris wheel in the world at the time, holding 1,200 people. Sometime later, I found an article in *Antique Trader* magazine about this Ferris wheel and how it was displayed at the World's Fair.

Being a subscriber of *Antique Trader* for many years, I cut out the Ferris wheel article and placed it with the paperweight. Sometime later, an antiques dealer came along and purchased my paperweight and writeup on the Ferris wheel for $200. I believe the excellent writeup about the wheel from *Antique Trader* was a large help in selling the weight.

— **Anthony Bontomase**
Pulaski, N.Y.

DEALER FINDS HIDDEN HISTORY ON HER FIRST DAY

• • • • • • • • •

It was my first day as a vendor in an antiques mall. I was waiting for months to get in, so when I got the call that a case was available, I grabbed the chance.

I spent a few days selecting what to bring. At the last minute, I decided on a snow painting. I had it in the basement for years and figured it was a snowy winter and someone would want it. The day I was setting up my case, two vendors approached me to welcome me to the mall.

In conversation, I mentioned that the most difficult task as a new vendor was to figure out how to price an item, for example, the snow painting I had purchased years ago at an antiques mall. I wasn't sure of the medium or what it was worth.

They suggested scratching off my label at the bottom of the painting to see if there was a signature, so I could say it was an "original." There was no signature. They waved goodbye, and now I was stuck with my label half on and half off. I began to scratch at the torn label when out from between the back of the painting and the front of it fell a photograph. It was in sepia tones, so it was hard to distinguish. A nearby customer identified the signature as Edward Curtis and the photo of American Indians. The woman said she was interested in buying it. I told her I needed to do a little research first. She said she would shop around and wait for me to return.

I went into the mall office and we Googled Edward Curtis. Pages and pages rolled off the printer and on the cover page was my photograph, "The Vanishing Race," Navajo Indians 1904. As it turned out, Edward Curtis photographed American Indians, beginning in the early 1900s, for more than 30 years in what was known as the North American Indian Project. His goal was to capture Native American culture in photo before it disappeared. "Vanishing Race" was Curtis' signature piece and reflected his concern.

My photo ended up being a platinum print and in very good condition. If I had not scratched at the torn label, I never would have known about the treasure buried inside and would have sold the snow painting for $35. In the end, I decided not to sell the photograph. I had it appraised, restored and properly framed. It now hangs on the wall in my home. I feel like I found a piece of American history that day. It has been a continuing adventure.

It is thrilling each time I tell the story. As a women in the mall said, "Some dealers wait a lifetime for a find. You did it the first day, and now you are done." It is by far my find of a lifetime.

— **Lynn Weitz**
Deerfield, Ill.

HALLOWEEN TREATS
• • • • • • • • •

"When I grow up, I want to be a rag picker."

Who plans that? What a fun way to make a buck! Although the term "treasure hunter" has a better ring to it.

My favorite treasure find (so far) was Halloween collectibles.

I was rag picking/treasure hunting at the local auction. After it ends every Tuesday afternoon and the buyers have sorted and taken what they want, they leave the rest all over the floor of a huge building — lots and lots of junk, and maybe ... treasure.

So I'm going through boxes (we call it rooting), and there are maybe only five pickers left in the building when I spot some Halloween and Christmas ornaments in the bottom of a box. I whisper to my partner, "SCORE!"

She says, "Why are you whispering? No one else here speaks English."

Found were two sets of composite candy containers made in Germany (1920s?); two pumpkins and a cat stacked on top of each other; one witch and one cat on little paper platforms with Germany stamped on the bottom; and 16 witch stickers. I'm so glad I found and saved them. They were minutes from going into the dumpster!

I put them on eBay in two lots starting at $9.99. In seven days, one lot sold for $423 and the other $349. How fun is that?

— **Sally Neal**
Molalla, Ore.

CELLULOID MICKEY MADE HER DAY

We were at the Peoria Doll Show in the early 1980s, and there was a flea market next door. We had finished setting up our booth, so we decided to take in the flea market. I couldn't believe my eyes. At one booth there was a 1934 Mickey Mouse celluloid windup in half of the original box!

It was perfect, with the Walt Disney stickers still in it and no dents in the celluloid. It was priced at $30. I exclaimed, "$30!" and the dealer thought he had priced it too high, so he said, "$27?"

I still have my little Mickey, and the last I heard, some like it were selling in the four-digit range.

— **Marge Meisinger**
Naperville, Ill.

THE JOY OF THE CHASE MATTERS MOST

I have two favorite yard-sale finds. The most recent purchase at a yard sale was a Kosta Boda candlestick signed "K." I purchased it for $2 and sold it to someone in Australia for $28.80.

The second find were two Wallace Nutting prints I purchased for $2, and they were sold at auction for $75.

I won't get wealthy, but the chase is fun.

— **Carole Stabile**
Wolfeboro, N.H.

DESK FIND SCORES POINTS WITH MOTHER-IN-LAW

Many years ago, when I lived in London, England, I was already a collector of small antiques and collectibles. I am now 86 years old and still collecting.

One Saturday afternoon, I heard the Boy Scouts were having a jumble (garage) sale. Now that was the very best, as it always was amazing what people give to the Scouts. It was in the Scout Hut, and it was packed. Well, I looked to see what I could find, and after a few minutes I saw the bottom half of a travel desk in good condition. I just had to get a hand on it through the pushing crowd. I managed with a bit of a shove to get hold of it and held tight. Now I had to find the top half!

Well, I looked and pushed, and I looked some more. Suddenly I saw a woman coming toward me, clutching the top half to her chest. We both looked at each other and, well, we both wanted what the other had! I offered to buy it from her and she also offered to do the same; neither gave in!

So, nearly desperate, I said, "PLEASE let me have it! It's for my mother-in-law who is visiting from Canada!" (Which was true). When she heard "mother-in-law," she looked at me and said, "Here, have it!"

And she was gone, and I had both halves!

I gave it to my mother-in-law, who took it to Canada and had it restored to its original beauty. I saw it years later when I visited. It had pride of place, and I silently thanked that unknown woman!

This is my most noteworthy story.

— **Lilli Arnoni**
via e-mail

RADIO BUFF LANDS
THE FIND OF A LIFETIME

• • • • • • • • •

I collect early vintage transistor radios, among other things. On weekends, I often spend mornings exploring our local (Denver) outdoor flea market, if for no other reason than to get a little fresh air and exercise and to swap stories with some of the other local collectors.

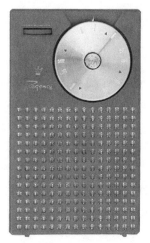

This market is a huge general flea market, which occupies several acres, and it is not unusual to see most anything for sale, including hot tubs, auto parts, fruits and vegetables, hand-crafted items, clothing, antiques, collectibles, and other assorted "junque." Once in a while, even a collectible radio shows up, although not nearly as frequently as most of us would hope! In the spirit of friendly competition, several of the local radio collectors anxiously await the rare opportunity to "pounce" on a collectible set!

One summer Saturday a few years ago, I was making my rounds through the flea market and experiencing my typical frustration due to lack of success in finding anything of interest. It was now mid-morning, and since it was a clear day, the mercury was already soaring. Given my total lack of success, I was beginning to question my sanity in continuing to search for anything on the flea market's large expanse of baking asphalt. After already having walked a few miles that morning, my feet were sore, and I was seriously considering abandoning the day's effort and instead engaging in more productive pursuits, such as going home and mowing the lawn.

"Ah," I figured, "One more round of the flea market couldn't hurt." All of a sudden, my heart nearly stopped.

From a distance, I spotted an item on one vendor's table that looked very familiar, almost at an instinctive level. Nah, it couldn't be. But the gold dial was in the right place. No, it would have been already snapped up by this late in the morning. Something in my gut told me I needed to see this item up close — and quickly.

To this day, I still can't recall how I got to the table, whether I simply ran or actually flew through the air. In a matter of seconds, I was holding a red, Regency TR-1 transistor radio in my hands, which I was able to purchase for the total sum of one dollar! My hands were shaking so hard, I could barely retrieve my billfold and present the money to the seller!

For those unfamiliar with vintage radios, the Regency TR-1 is the very first commercially produced transistor radio. The TR-1 first came to market in the fall of 1954, at the hefty price of nearly $50, making it expensive for the typical consumer back then. The introduction of this Regency pocket radio really did begin the headlong rush into developing and marketing portable electronic devices that are so prevalent today. As "the first," these radios are highly sought-after today and command a premium price from both radio collectors and students of technology history.

The Regency TR-1 is on display at the Smithsonian and in many other collections displaying the most significant breakthroughs in applying technology to meet consumer needs.

The radio I found that morning a few years back is not quite in perfect shape, yet it is exhibited proudly on my shelf as a treasured item in my collection.

I'm personally convinced that the sequence of events I have described here and the ultimate triumph in finding this radio are every bit as important to me as the actual possession of the radio. In other words, I would not have experienced nearly as much fun if I had simply purchased the radio from another collector for big bucks.

So, to all of my fellow collectors, the dream remains alive!

You, too, could come across that ultimate treasure when you least expect it!

— **Neil Gallensky**
Westminster, Colo.

KOREAN MASK A SPECIAL FIND

• • • • • • • • •

My favorite find is this Korean traditional mask in a frame, in its original box. Every month my husband and I travel 38 miles to Victorville, Calif., to a thrift shop on senior citizen's day.

— **Johnnie and Marie Turner**
Barstow, Calif.

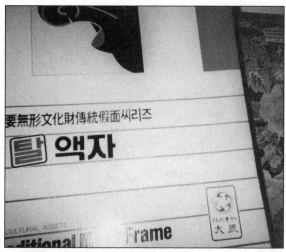

This 1949 Cadillac is much like the one the letter writer describes.

VINTAGE WHEELS BRING JOY

• • • • • • • •

When I was 15, in 1968, my dad went to a farm sale. It was raining, so he got inside a car that was in the sale. He turned on the key and pushed the starter button, and it started. He paid $82 for it and was offered $200 to sell it before he left the sale to bring it home. It was a 1949 Cadillac with less than 50,000 miles on it. The farmer/veterinarian who owned it had gone to Detroit and picked it up for his wife. She only drove it around the small rural town where they lived. She had a German shepherd that rode in the back seat. My dad thought it would be safe car for me to drive because it was kinda like driving a tank. I hauled a lot of kids in it during my high school years. Not many kids had cars back then.

When I was married, my husband, little boy and I camped in it at the lake. In my college speech class, I wrote a speech about it for "One of the Smartest Things I Ever Bought." Needless to say, I received an A. Everyone was amazed that it had an ivory steering wheel, huge chrome bumpers, push-button starter and to fill the gas tank, you pushed a button on the taillight. When my son was 16, he was going to paint it white with flames. The original color was an army green. It sat stripped down for almost 25 years. We are now in the process of restoring it to the original color. It was one of the cheapest best buys we ever made and just accidently ran across it. I do not plan on selling it and don't really know its value. I can't wait to drive it again with my grandkids.

— **Jera Swartz,**
Granby, Mo.

PARKER 'SNAKE' GETS NEW HOME

· · · · · · · · ·

In 1975, I was a young physician in my first year of practice with a young wife, two young children and plenty of free time because the practice was not that busy yet. I already had a passion for timepieces and had a small ad in the local newspaper advertising my interest in acquiring old watches. One afternoon I received a call from an older gentleman who said he had a few pocket watches and was wondering if I would be interested. He did not know what he had and was not an expert, but he was willing to show them to me and was open to a reasonable offer.

It was a 30-minute drive, and I decided to take a ride to see the watches. As it often happens, they were not of the collectible quality, even if they were old. After looking at the movements, I decided to pass. My host felt sorry I had taken that long trip for naught. He was apologetic, and on my way out asked if I was interested in other old objects. He had a bag of old pens and had heard that people were collecting old pens. I was not that interested in old pens, but I had a few that I had previously picked here and there and I accepted the offer to look at them. He then brought out a small cigar box half filled with old pens. One quick look showed me some Shaeffers, Parkers and a few Watermans. He wanted $100 for the lot, and on a whim I decided to buy them. As collectors know, it's almost unheard of for us to go all primed up to an antiques-buying expedition, auction, garage sale etc., and come home empty handed.

Back at the office, I had a few patients' calls to take care of, and I deposited the box of pens in a drawer down the basement. I then totally forgot about them.

Almost six years later, pen collecting took a sharp upward turn. Mr. Cliff Lawrence of Florida, the godfather of pen collecting, started writing articles about fountain pens, and Parker BIG REDS became an instant celebrity in the collecting world. He wrote monthly articles concerning different old pens, and one of those articles caught my attention. Mr. Lawrence was describing a pen he called "Parker Snake." It was an early pen, the kind named eye droppers because the ink was instilled into the pen reservoir just that way. Mr. Lawrence described it as a smallish, elegant pen, with intertwined metallic snakes with emerald green eyes on the body. The nib was gold. According to him such a pen was very rare, desirable, and valued at $7,500.

It was a revelation. I never thought of pens as having that enormous value. I then remembered the ones I had stored in the basement so long ago and decided to have a closer look at them. I was not thinking Parker Snake, but perhaps a Big Red or a Parker 51 could be found — at least I was hoping.

I went down the basement and pulled the pens out. And there, in all its splendor, was a Parker Snake. It was in as good a condition as you could ever find an old pen and did not appear to have been used. The remaining pens were just old ordinary Parkers, Shaeffers, Esterbrooks, etc.

In 2000, I suffered a stroke, and I stopped practicing medicine and surgery. In

2001, my family needed money, and we decided to sell the pen on a new selling medium called eBay. It brought $25,000 and found a new home in the pocket of a radiologist in Singapore.

— **Roger Maleche, MD, FACS.**
Broadalbin, N.Y.

AUCTION FIND TURNS OUT TO BE RARE SHONA SCULPTURE

• • • • • • • •

For several years until the auction house closed, my wife and I would attend a weekly auction in St. Petersburg, Fla. Typically this auction house, which often handled more run-of-the-mill items and estate liquidations, would sometimes include some nice items. We have purchased and sold our share of things, but

one item that we purchased surpassed anything that we had bought before or since.

One week, the auction house had some "Shona" sculptures: stone carvings from various Zimbabwe artisans. Like most stone sculptures, they were heavy, and some were signed with names of people no one had ever heard of! The auction house published an online listing of some of its items a few days before the auction, and we happened to see some photos of the several stone sculptures in one picture. There were six or seven in total, as I recall. They were not attributed to any artist, but they looked interesting and might look good as a decorative item in our home, if the price was cheap enough. It wasn't something we needed, but just something that would be nice to have. Our home is populated by many pieces of Victorian furniture, so Shona sculptures would be a nice contrast to those things and perhaps make our home more eclectic.

Before going out to the auction to view the items before the sale, I did a brief

Google search for Shona sculpture and Zimbabwe artists. I hoped to at least get some awareness of what to look for in stone sculptures, what types of stone might be used, and perhaps some basic information on the people who carved them. I also tried to find out about prices for such items by looking on eBay and discovered that most items sold for under $150. That sounded like our price range, so we decided that if one or more of the stone sculptures were attractive to us and reasonably priced, we would buy one or a few of them.

We followed our normal pattern by going out to the auction house about three hours before the start of the auction, looking over what was being offered, and then going out for dinner. We would normally arrive back at the auction house about 30 minutes prior to the start of the auction and pick out our seats. We liked three or four of the stone sculptures and marked them for bidding when they came up for auction. Most of them were not at the beginning of the auction, so we would have to wait for quite a while before they would be available for bid. Normally, we don't wait around, because we don't want to get home too late in the evening, but we decided that we would stay out a bit later to see what prices these stone sculptures would bring. We bid on some other items, although I don't really remember what they were (we typically bought a few things, such as jewelry, small furniture pieces and lower-priced artwork).

The Shona sculptures finally came up for bidding, and amazingly, no one seemed to want them, except for another individual who was a regular at the auction and who purchased items for resale in a retail shop. The opening bid was low, something like $20, as I remember. A few people bid at the lower prices, which was normal for this auction (people would bid low prices for the chance at acquiring something dirt cheap). Soon, only we and this regular bidder were bidding on these items. When the price for the first stone sculpture reached a few hundred dollars, we decided that it was too much to pay, and we stopped bidding. A second sculpture came up, which we liked a bit more than the first one, so we bid on it. Again, the only serious bidder was the retail shop owner seeking items for resale. This time, the item sold for a more reasonable price, and we were the high bidder! That was kind of nice! Feeling more confident now that we might not get outbid on every Shona piece being offered for sale, we determined that there were two other pieces that we most preferred, and we would go a bit higher if need be to outbid our main competitor. In total, we purchased three pieces that evening, with prices ranging from $150 to $250 (plus buyer's premium).

We loaded our purchases up at the end of the auction, and boy, they were heavy! I'm not getting any younger or stronger, but we managed to get them loaded into our car and head for home. As I normally do, the next day I examined our purchases in more detail and started to do some Internet searches for more information about the items. Each stone sculpture was signed by an artist, so I began my search. For the first piece, I could find nothing about the artist at all — probably sculpted by someone along the side of the road that sold these pieces to tourists and made a living that way. The second piece had an artist's name, and I assumed that my search would again prove fruitless. Amazingly, the artist's name came up in my search. Now, it was time to find out who this person was. The artist was John Takawira. I read about how he was considered the father of Shona sculpture in his country, and that he had sons also involved in the profession. It mentioned that he had passed away several years before, and that his sculptures could be found in many museums and galleries in Africa, Europe and the United States. I was impressed that we had purchased something we liked, and it had been created by a well-known artist. We assumed that all of the stone sculptures we purchased were likely made by nondescript artists, and they would only be worth what we had paid for them (or perhaps less). When we found out that one of them was by a well-known artist, we decided to seek out some expert advice.

By coincidence, the "Antiques Roadshow" was coming to Tampa (where we live), and we had obtained tickets to it earlier and could bring two items for appraisal. One of the two items we decided to take to the show was the John Takawira stone sculpture. We went to the show excited that they might be able to tell us something about the item and to tell us what it might be worth. What a disappointment! The "expert" there knew nothing about Shona sculpture or the artist and could offer no opinion as to the value of the item.

So, after returning home, in the next month or so we were able to locate someone who knew something about Shona sculptures and could provide some estimate of its value. Well, we had the item appraised and amazingly, received an appraisal for

$15,000 for insurance purposes. Knowing that insurance appraisals are high, we asked what the piece could sell for if placed in an auction of African items. They indicated that because of the artist's name and excellent condition of the sculpture, it would probably bring $7,000 to $8,000, or perhaps more if several people wanted the same piece.

We were not really interested in selling the item, since we had bought it because we liked it. It now is proudly displayed in our home (in a safe place so as not to get "dinged"). It represents our best ever purchase with a return on our investment of 2,800 percent (based on a possible selling price of $7,000 and our purchase price of $250). If we never achieve such a result again, we're still happy. Nothing could surpass this!

— **James and Katheryn Stock**
Lutz, Fla.

WHEN IT COMES TO FUN, CHILDHOOD SWAMP HUNTS TRUMP ANTIQUING

· · · · · · · ·

I am 84 years old; 72 years ago, when I was 12, I used to go treasure hunting. I lived about a mile or two from where they had dumped the debris from the 1906 earthquake. This was close to the San Francisco Bay, but quite a ways from San Francisco. I lived in a little town called Clyde, Calif., that had only one small grocery store. We took the train to school.

Our most fun was taking gunny sacks and hiking through the swamps to where the relics from the earthquake were. We would find old iron toys. I remember an old iron toy fire engine drawn by horses, and a 1903 license plate. Our sacks would be pretty heavy to carry home, and it was a long hike through the swamps. My mother would tell us to quit bringing home all this junk. When we moved, I guess it was all thrown out! How I wish I had it now.

It's funny that I can remember it so vividly, like it was yesterday, but I have a hard time remembering what I did this morning. I have bought and sold antiques and collectibles for many years since then. I don't think hunting treasures was ever more fun than our hikes with gunny sacks through the swamps.

— **Pat Rebello**
Eagle Point, Ore.

TYPESETTER'S CHEST HOLDS MORE THAN A PRACTICAL PURPOSE
• • • • • • • • •

We were on the way to a wedding in the cornfields of southern Illinois, traveling in the van owned by college friends and devoted antiquers. Our progress was slow, impeded by stops at every shop or mall visible from the highway.

My husband and I trailed behind, not intending to buy but merely to look. Oh! Oh! There is was! In a crowded mall in uncharted countryside, buried deep in a dark corner, heaped with boxes and a huge rug, was a typesetter's chest.

The top was stained with ink, and each of its 15 drawers bore testament to its lifelong function. It was a heavy oak piece, created from slabs of wood; yet all 15 numbered drawers slid in and out easily. We exchanged significant looks. The price was right, somewhere over $100, we were riding in a roomy vehicle, and best of all, not one but two young and strong men were in our party. To our friends' amazement, we bought the chest and staggered to position it for the round trip ride to the Quonset hut wedding of a goddaughter.

Once at home, Frank removed all of the inserts, which fortunately lifted out easily, took them apart and sanded each piece. He cleaned the drawer bottoms and lined them with pale blue velvet before reinserting the partitions, then removed the top, thinking to replace it with a marble slab.

The chest became the repository for all the costume jewelry owned by one slightly offbeat Spanish teacher — me. It sat for years without a top until finally Frank went to the garage, reclaimed the original boards, and ink stains and all, replaced them on the chest.

This has been one of the most practical items we ever purchased; it rests comfortably among companion stoneware and banks. Its drawers are filled with like items: earrings with birds, silver Mexican pins, beaded necklaces ... all items essential for classroom appearances. There is even a pin and matching earrings presented by a dear fellow teacher and inveterate phone chatter, naturally in the shape of telephones.

And, in case I forget to mention, the typesetter's chest holds fond memories of my father, a printer who carried the perfumed scent of ink wherever he went.

— **Vicky Kellen**
Castle Pines, Colo.

POKER CHIP RACK HAS BIG PAYOUT
· · · · · · · · ·

Six years ago, I visited a thrift store in Camarillo, Calif., where I found a large revolving poker-chip rack. It was made of walnut and filled with vintage clay chips. I thought the chips and rack may be of some value, so I purchased the set for $18.

I asked the manager to contact me if any other poker chips came into the shop. A week later, she called informing me another rack with clay chips had arrived. This was a smaller rack made from what I believed to be Bakelite. It contained 20 clay chips of different varieties. I purchased this set for $10.

The first rack contained 270 chips, mostly in excellent condition, but in need of cleaning after many years of use. The additional 20 from the smaller rack needed cleaning, as well.

So, there I sat for days, cleaning 290 chips! In my mind's eye, I imagined the many poker games that had taken place and folks that had used them. Probably a lot of good stories there ... if only those chips could talk!

Eventually, I sold both sets and even sold several chips separately. I found through research, that the Shamrock "Good Luck" clay chips and the "Bulldog" chips were highly regarded by collectors. I got a few e-mails asking if I had access to more of these chips. Boy! I wish I had, that's for sure.

My total purchases came to $28, and I sold the racks and chips for $425, a profit of $397!

These chips were one of my best finds ever, and I'm still searching for more. Not likely though, after reading your article (Sept. 7, 2011, edition) on the big poker chip find in Nevada! Oh well, I can still dream ...

Love the Antique Trader and especially the "Favorite Finds" contest.

— **Regards,**
Georgia Dupuis
Townville, S.C.

RING WORTH WAY MORE
THAN 75 GUM WRAPPERS
· · · · · · · · ·

I was digging through old boxes of toys at an estate sale, and the woman running the sale walks in and holds up her pinky and says, "Anyone want a Tom Mix ring?" I say sure. I buy it for $10, and it sits in my box of stuff to go through (eventually) for six months.

When I look at it I realize it is a Tom Mix Deputy Ring, issued for one year in 1934, only if you bought and saved 75 wrappers of T.M. Gum, and, I think, 10 cents and sent it in quickly. Well, not too many exist, and the one I had was in great shape. I tried to put a realistic price on it in the antiques mall I am in and it sat for two years. I then put it into a Hakes auction, where it realized $5,600. Was I happy or what? That's my great find!

— **Andrew "Marty" Martin**
via e-mail

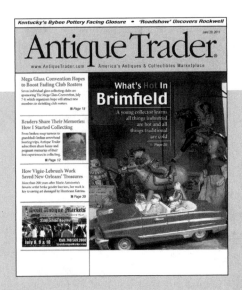